Thank you for purchasing our Crossword    ⌐κ!

Inside you will find 90 puzzles with solutions at the back.

We are a very small team and we always review our books before publishing, however its possible that new releases may contain small mistakes that we have missed. If you find a mistake in any of our books please contact us immediately so we can fix the issue as soon as possible.

**CrosswordPanda@gmail.com**

# No. 1

## Across

**1.** 'Alternatively ...,' in texts
**5.** Bake-off figure
**9.** Big name in food service
**14.** Agnew's plea, briefly
**15.** Attachment to "nautics" or "dynamic"
**16.** A storm might knock it out
**17.** Dialogue between diner waitresses?
**20.** Delicate mushrooms
**21.** A.S.A.P. in an E.R.
**22.** 'A Theory of Semiotics' author
**23.** Honey eater of New Zealand
**25.** Ace's objective
**26.** Altoids container
**27.** One who gets bent out of shape
**33.** Be abrasive on
**34.** River to the Rhône
**35.** Chaka who sang with Rufus
**37.** A singer can carry one
**38.** Acid + alcohol compound
**41.** Actor Jack of oaters
**43.** Babe in a barn
**45.** 'Cap'n ___' (1904 novel)
**46.** Dept. that works with Sales
**47.** They present hurdles
**51.** Accuse of negligence, perhaps
**53.** Ariz. neighbor
**54.** Apres-___
**55.** Abbr. on a key
**56.** Practice, practice, practice
**58.** Alluringly slender
**63.** Soak up the sun, say
**66.** A chorus line
**67.** A celebrity carries one
**68.** Act of digitization
**69.** Start of an African capital
**70.** Apply spin
**71.** Bird's home: Var.

## Down

**1.** A Grimm beginning?
**2.** Animated character
**3.** Author Ijeoma
**4.** Alert for a distracted driver
**5.** Pauses in poetry
**6.** 'And I Love ___'
**7.** Accentuated periods
**8.** How a tandem bicycle is built
**9.** First launch in the space race
**10.** Day, to Dayan
**11.** Wheedles
**12.** 'The ___: A Tragedy in Five Acts' (Shelley work)
**13.** 'Funeral Games' playwright
**18.** A brother of Michael Jackson
**19.** Acquire
**24.** Ailment ending
**27.** Portion of a ton: Abbr.
**28.** Egg: Fr
**29.** Time in which light travels one foot, approximately
**30.** Alternative to 'trick' on Halloween
**31.** Becomes wearisome
**32.** Jewish pledge of faith
**36.** Archibald of NBA fame
**39.** Spanish for 'you are'
**40.** Two-wheeled transport
**42.** Autos originally from Oxford
**44.** University speakers
**48.** A katydid's are found on its legs, strangely enough
**49.** Acapulco beaches
**50.** Apiary unit
**51.** Anatomical dividers
**52.** Did some theater work, casually
**57.** Singular of 'Inuit'
**59.** Early weather satellite
**60.** Adult nits
**61.** Russian autocrat: Var.
**62.** Children's rhyme starter
**64.** French 'you'
**65.** A third of nove

# No. 2

## Across

1. Pakistan divider
6. Beginning to care?
10. Brief bylaws
14. Cathedral city of Tuscany
15. Alphabetically first former Crown colony
16. A friend in need
17. Former lover's text, e.g.?
20. A. A. Milne baby
21. A Gabor
22. Delaware Indian
23. Along the way
26. Any of nine inspirational goddesses
27. Like some diplomatic roles
32. Call for
34. Aid the chef
35. Conductance unit
36. Been abed
37. Annual pageant winner
38. Capital ENE of Fiji
39. Chicago columnist Kupcinet
40. Actress Elisabeth
42. Aching the most
44. UNDERLINE
47. Knights' titles in 'A Game of Thrones'
48. Double-___
51. Iranian president Rouhani
54. Kipling's 'wary old python'
55. Actress Munson of 'Gone With the Wind'
56. Like some antennae
60. Amazon and Orinoco, to natives
61. Alias for H. H. Munro
62. Batter's place
63. Adult eft
64. Classic TV's "___-Team"
65. After-Christmas events

## Down

1. Alpine feeder
2. 'A Quiet Passion' actress Cynthia
3. Like some arts
4. A tenth of diez
5. Actor/musician Milby
6. Shades of purple
7. Actress Best
8. 'Ad majorem ___ gloriam' (Jesuit motto)
9. Make room for
10. Brett who directed 'Rush Hour'
11. 'All Fools' Day' essayist
12. Definitely not haute cuisine
13. Ago, in a seasonal song
18. A Band Called Pain music genre
19. Ancient master of didacticism
24. A sultanate
25. Quaestor's question
26. Big red planet
28. Mary Anne in "The Baby-Sitters Club"
29. Q: Do you gossip? A: Yes. ___
30. Large food tunas
31. Experimental fashion?
32. Director Petri
33. Antidrug agent, informally
37. Acts clownishly
38. Aggressive god
40. Four-time Vardon Trophy winner
41. Brass instrument player
42. Anchovy or sand eel
43. "Ah, I see"
45. Alley-oop pass, maybe
46. Australia's national blossom
49. A maternal relation
50. Abnormal respiratory sounds
51. A driver may lay on it
52. Beau's girl
53. April or November surprise
54. Actress/TV host Palmer
57. A bit of cheer?
58. Computer addresses, for short
59. Brazilian greeting

# No. 3

## Across

1. Brokerage house T. ___ Price
5. Scanty, in London
11. Actor/rapper ___ Def
14. 'A Summer Place' co-star
15. Attorney Gloria
16. Abused opioid, for short
17. Radio D.J., e.g
19. 'A friend to call my own,' per a Michael Jackson hit
20. Cancel, as a fine
21. Actress Dobrev of 'The Vampire Diaries'
22. Mag. publisher's concern
23. Helper on a horse farm
25. Act like Pavlov's dogs
27. Former western English county
32. Abbr. appropriate for JFK and LAX
33. Acted like a sap?
34. 'Aren't you forgetting something?'
38. 'Beowulf' and others
41. Arroyo ___ (Rose Bowl setting)
42. Ambrosian Library setting
44. Cancellation stamp
46. Deplorably cowardly
51. Bob preceder
52. Debate club fodder
55. Actor Gooding Jr
57. A metrical unit
60. Decorated athlete whose name could be parsed as 'zero' + 'loss'
61. Abbr. in the White House address
62. Like infighting
64. Aachen article
65. Baseball Hall-of-Famer Fox
66. A kid may be told to watch it
67. A facelift removes it
68. Escapee from a witch in a Grimm tale
69. A Rice Krispies fellow

## Down

1. Camera-ready page
2. Arches in Gothic architecture
3. Amiable quality
4. Do a farm chore
5. Any chess piece
6. Anagram of lean
7. 'And ___ ask is a tall ship ...': John Masefield
8. Dating app
9. Delay development
10. Big name in confectioneries
11. Put into action
12. Hedge with a guardrail to contain livestock
13. Adjust to match, informally
18. Cheri formerly of 'S.N.L'
22. Aquatic silvers
24. Actor Auberjonois
26. Animal in un zoológico
28. Modern way to transfer documents
29. Antipasto bit
30. A little fun?
31. Base of the Tokugawa shoguns
34. A Vanderbilt
35. Belt along
36. Analyst who leaked the Pentagon Papers
37. Michelle and Barack's elder daughter
39. Army VIP
40. Alluvial deposit
43. Agatha Christie's '___ M?'
45. A moon of Saturn
47. Apt surname for a hot dog vendor?
48. Any of the Fab Four
49. Periods added to harmonize the lunar and solar calendars
50. Joan who wrote 'The Year of Magical Thinking'
53. Flowering tropical plant
54. A buzzer may end it
55. Bad boyfriends
56. Bit of eye makeup?
58. Alternative to a B.L.T.
59. A French cheese
62. Amsterdam-based financial co
63. Bellini's '___ furor delle tempeste'

# No. 4

## Across

1. Comment of indifference
5. Amenhotep IV's god
9. Bar rooms?
14. Actress Falana
15. Ancient Roman costume
16. A genius, no
17. Gun-toting Annie
18. Another name for it is 'moonfish'
19. Mexico's ___ Laredo
20. Everyday
23. Actress ___ Scala
24. Buys on time?
25. Afire with desire
27. Chewed like a beaver
30. Algerian currency
32. Actor Cariou
33. Friml operetta with the song 'Indian Love Call'
37. Not sufficiently concerned about
41. Alternative to tarot cards
42. Env. alternative
43. Displaces from an overbooked flight
44. Computer company with the slogan 'Imagine it. Done.'
47. Beyond that
50. A freelancer may work on it
51. A dog's ___ (long spell)
52. Norah O'Donnell, e.g
58. Southern gospel group the ___ Family
60. Acronym akin to 'carpe diem'
61. Absolutely nothing
62. Turkish leader Atatürk
63. Athos, Porthos and Aramis
64. Nickname for Isabelle or Isidore
65. Actress Davis of the 'Matrix' movies
66. Abnormal enlargement
67. Average grades

## Down

1. Aligned group
2. Olympic hurdler/bobsledder Jones
3. B or C, but not A or D: Abbr.
4. Barn area
5. Did penance
6. Bazooka Joe's company
7. Alike, in Paris
8. Capital of Okinawa
9. Film-related anagram of AMERICAN
10. Academic address ender
11. Belgian burg
12. 'Good ___' (1966 Young Rascals hit)
13. Animal that's a little weaselly?
21. Are borrowers
22. Cave ___
26. Alternative to hell?
27. Engorge
28. A goose on the Hawaiian Islands
29. All that ___ bag of chips
30. Acts feebleminded
31. 'Aida' chorus subject
33. Accept an invitation
34. Bad things for astronaut suits to have
35. Appropriate name for a pet squid?
36. A robin's are blue
38. Czech Republic river
39. Eco-friendly, perhaps
40. Former Irish P.M. ___ de Valera
44. Rebelled
45. Ad catchword
46. Bigger-than-life
47. Artist August ___ of the Blaue Reiter school
48. Baddies
49. Amounts of paper
50. A state of matter
53. Blue in printer cartridges
54. Cato's man
55. Big garden project
56. A woodworker wields it
57. Ayes' antitheses
59. Actress ___ Ling of 'Sky Captain and the World of Tomorrow'

# No. 5

## Across

**1.** Audio boosters

**5.** Actress Kate of 'Grey's Anatomy'

**10.** Unit of frequency

**13.** Abraded

**14.** Apparently amazed

**15.** A gun, slangily

**16.** River that's the site of Javert's demise in 'Les Misérables'

**17.** Allowed by law

**18.** A Freud

**19.** Job mistakenly sought by a TV addict?

**22.** Actress Phillipa

**24.** Atty. ___

**25.** Articles of merchandise

**26.** One who engages in finger painting

**31.** Internal obstruction

**32.** A large amount

**33.** 'And our love become a funeral ___' (lyric from the Doors' 'Light My Fire')

**34.** Branch wannabes

**36.** Jebel ___ (Moroccan mountain)

**40.** Contemporary sweethearts

**41.** 'April Theses' writer

**42.** Hazarding a guess: doughy metaphysician?

**47.** Versace rival

**48.** Acronym associated with retirement?

**49.** Caesar's force

**50.** Capable of being decomposed

**55.** 'A person who talks when you wish him to listen,' per Ambrose Bierce

**56.** Certain family members, affectionately

**57.** Dinner crumbs

**60.** Galway Bay islands

**61.** Break a deadlock

**62.** Cinder-covered

**63.** Dict. demarcation

**64.** Be upright

**65.** Animal fare

## Down

**1.** Comments around babies

**2.** Alpine skier Tommy

**3.** Hoosegow occupant

**4.** Already in the mail

**5.** Great Scott

**6.** Getting on

**7.** Body of agua

**8.** Airplane wing measure

**9.** Ahab's post

**10.** Middle of Manchester

**11.** Cheese sometimes served with saag

**12.** All-___

**15.** Comedian Minhaj

**20.** A long stretch

**21.** Amazes

**22.** Act like a faulty CD

**23.** Acne-prone

**27.** Adequate

**28.** Discriminator against the elderly

**29.** Baseball's Maris, for short

**30.** Airer of N.C.A.A. March Madness games

**34.** An ideal, in Chinese philosophy

**35.** Benign bump

**36.** A Little Woman

**37.** All there is

**38.** 'Absolutely!' in Acapulco

**39.** 'A Bug's Life' bugs

**40.** Caesar's "well"

**41.** Bausch & ___

**42.** Home to monks or nuns

**43.** Ethically challenged

**44.** Afflicted (with)

**45.** Admit to the clergy

**46.** Chartered

**47.** Arafat successor

**51.** African beasts

**52.** Act the demagogue

**53.** Architectural pier

**54.** Act like a couch potato

**58.** A cousin?

**59.** Actor Chaplin, Charlie's older brother

# No. 6

## Across

**1.** Actor Arnold

**4.** Bluff formed by a fault

**9.** Hon, modern-style

**12.** A way to pray or read

**15.** Home of Jar Jar Binks in 'Star Wars' films

**16.** Adj. modifier

**17.** City in Texas

**18.** Math coordinates

**20.** Emmy-winning role for Sally Field

**21.** Actor Gregory of 'To Kill a Mockingbird'

**22.** Not his'n

**23.** Altar exchanges

**25.** How some wine is sold

**27.** Cornea neighbor

**30.** Affected intellectual

**31.** Blender noise

**32.** Big workday for Saint Nick

**34.** Annual CBS awards broadcast, with 'the'

**38.** Accelerator bits

**39.** 'Get Yer ___ Out!' (1970 live album)

**41.** Braided

**42.** City bonds, informally

**44.** Adjust, as a clock

**45.** 'Dawson's Creek' star James Van Der ___

**46.** Adhering to Strunk and White's advice 'Omit needless words'

**48.** Big, in Bari

**50.** Angle that just isn't right

**53.** Barnum's 'Feejee Mermaid,' e.g

**54.** A river might run through it

**55.** Aeneas abandoned her

**57.** Little disagreements

**61.** Having two equal sides

**63.** A way to habituate

**64.** Archaic 'your'

**65.** German boulevard

**66.** Beehive State city

**67.** Evil general in 'Superman II'

**68.** Batik artisans

**69.** Appreciate, informally

## Down

**1.** A little night music?

**2.** Nonsense word repeated before 'oxen free'

**3.** Ancient Dead Sea kingdom

**4.** Alternative to buttons on a jacket

**5.** 'The Daughters of Joshua ___' (1972 Buddy Ebsen film)

**6.** Distances from the y-axis on a graph

**7.** Famed Notre Dame coach

**8.** Baked Hawaiian dish

**9.** A dinger gets you four

**10.** How a prank may be done, after 'on'

**11.** Balances (out)

**13.** They're staffed with doctors

**14.** Extreme sorrow

**19.** Form of sparring

**24.** Candlelike

**26.** Action before 'paste'

**27.** Come crawling back?

**28.** Ancient Chinese dynasty

**29.** Actor Mark ___-Baker

**30.** Cash recipient

**33.** 'The Count of Monte Cristo' setting

**35.** All those against

**36.** Actor Montand

**37.** Mobutu Sese ___, Zairian despot

**40.** Beehive State bloomer

**43.** Et ___ (abbr. meaning "and the following")

**47.** In an uncivil way

**49.** Batting average or body mass index

**50.** Ex-Disney chief Michael

**51.** Poet credited with popularizing haiku

**52.** Andrew ___ Webber

**53.** Certain gardening supplies

**56.** A buck or two?

**58.** Animated hunter Elmer

**59.** Costing nothing, in Cologne

**60.** Hong Kong's Hang ___ Index

**62.** Base man

## Across

**1.** Bones, anatomically
**5.** Business leader?
**9.** Elder Stark daughter on 'Game of Thrones'
**14.** Colored
**15.** Annual coronation site
**16.** AL West team
**17.** Embezzles, e.g
**20.** Acoustic term
**21.** Badly hurt
**22.** 'Are ___ pair?' ('Send in the Clowns' lyric)
**23.** A dunker may grab it
**25.** Batting coach Charley, who wrote 'The Art of Hitting .300'
**26.** A little strange
**27.** Job involving prediction
**33.** Kind of rm. for an R.N.
**34.** American Kennel Club designation
**35.** Actress Chase
**37.** Two-toed sloth
**38.** Boar or sow
**41.** Baltic capital
**43.** Actress Rae
**45.** Alternative to smoking
**46.** Albatross
**47.** Rulers
**51.** Appointment book pg.
**53.** Low-grade wool
**54.** A little resistance
**55.** Athlete in a shell
**56.** Bagasse base, maybe
**58.** Disorderly one
**63.** Big bang creator
**66.** Bedtime woe
**67.** 'A Life for the Tsar' hero Susanin
**68.** Aftertaste, e.g.
**69.** Access the internet, say
**70.** Bern is on it
**71.** Adirondack chair element

## Down

**1.** An omega might represent them
**2.** Attire for the boardroom
**3.** Former Zairian leader Mobutu ___ Seko
**4.** Certain Jewish month
**5.** Names
**6.** Angry dog's sound
**7.** B&B offering
**8.** Pierce through
**9.** Action preceders
**10.** Accusatory exclamation
**11.** Activity for Hollywood newbies
**12.** 'How We Fight for Our Lives' author Jones
**13.** Bashar of Syria
**18.** A neighbor of Chile
**19.** Balboa : Panama :: ___ : Iran
**24.** Abyssinian greeting
**27.** Blaze, to Blaise
**28.** All at the front?
**29.** Confidence-boosting
**30.** Be confident in
**31.** Binding things together
**32.** Scott of 'Men in Trees'
**36.** A fit of shivering
**39.** Area near Manhattan's Union Square
**40.** Install as king
**42.** A male one is a jack
**44.** Bedouin, say
**48.** Act as a henchman
**49.** Airline to Spain
**50.** Actor Jannings
**51.** Add up
**52.** Arthur Marx
**57.** 'L'Shana ___ ' (Rosh Hashanah greeting)
**59.** Alibis
**60.** A shade of blue
**61.** Central Sicilian city
**62.** Armory grp.
**64.** A new beginning?
**65.** Adhesive for feathers?

# No. 8

## Across

1. Asian gambling destination
6. Caribbean taro
10. Army locale
14. Babe in the woods
15. Drove diagonally
16. Austrian Expressionist Schiele
17. Upright basketball player?
20. Artist Gerard ___ Borch
21. A corrosive
22. Area of Venice
23. Certain Black Sea dweller
26. Activist Guinier
27. Apt to induce goose bumps
32. Bank (on)
34. Absorbs, as a loss
35. When doubled, a book by Gauguin
36. Adequate, in verse
37. Dad's namesake: Abbr.
38. Binge-watch, maybe
39. 'Atlas Shrugged' author Rand
40. Air apparent?
42. Eager (to go)
44. They have an unstable nucleus
47. Cellos, violas, etc.: Abbr.
48. Out of place, in obstetric parlance
51. Elton's 'Through the Storm' duettist
54. Army E-3
55. Clandestine maritime org
56. Organisms studiers
60. Fungal spore cases
61. Danish shoe brand
62. CBer's sign-offs
63. Bits of a song refrain
64. City northwest of Soissons
65. Bad time for a procrastinator

## Down

1. Breast: Prefix
2. Appeared on stage
3. Exchange letters
4. Altar constellation
5. A single opening?
6. Gas for welders
7. Act feeblemindedly
8. 'Absolutely,' for short
9. Aromatic additive to natural gas
10. Bawl over
11. 'I got ___ ...'
12. Alphabetize
13. High-quality cannabis, in slang
18. Endocrine or pituitary
19. Audi logo quartet
24. Belch forth
25. Act immorally
26. Ananias, famously
28. Indie rock band Yo La ___
29. Unwilling
30. Bright moment
31. Association of criminals
32. Alternative to "honey" or "sugar"
33. 'A Day Without Rain' artist
37. British singer Stone
38. After-dinner sandwich?
40. Bantu language group
41. Airport city near Montreal
42. Boxer Graziano, formally
43. A quick study
45. Montezuma and others
46. Cookware coating
49. IV component
50. Two-time Grammy winner Houston
51. Activist ___ Alamuddin Clooney
52. Laughter, in La Mancha
53. Book after Prov.
54. A little in Spain
57. Ancient royal
58. Acquired
59. Literature Nobelist Andric

# No. 9

## Across

**1.** A fish ... or to cook it, in a way

**5.** 'Chances Are' crooner Johnny

**11.** Abbr. before Friday

**14.** Physics Nobelist Isidor

**15.** Actress DeBose

**16.** Choice marble

**17.** How many practice religion

**19.** Abbr. after a price in a Craigslist ad

**20.** Any "Jurassic Park" dinosaur

**21.** Daughter of Atlas

**22.** Adds cubes, e.g

**23.** Post-Taliban Afghan president

**25.** Hudson River town

**27.** Novel that focuses on character growth

**32.** Aping avian

**33.** Camus's 'Lettres à ___ Allemand'

**34.** 'Ain't She Sweet' composer Milton

**38.** Cleo of jazz

**41.** Affront

**42.** Bar soap brand

**44.** Arctic Circle inhabitant

**46.** They make loud noises during showers

**51.** Cotton thread

**52.** Act like aloe

**55.** Dress ___ (impersonate)

**57.** Bit of ginger powder

**60.** Bit, as of evidence

**61.** A good thing to get out of

**62.** Some sushi menu fish

**64.** Andre Young a.k.a. Dr. ___

**65.** Air carrier based in Seoul

**66.** Act the layabout

**67.** A tot may have a big one

**68.** Like heists and operas

**69.** Actual

## Down

**1.** Earthenware pot

**2.** 'Se ___ espanol'

**3.** Act like a sponge

**4.** Early Wagner opera

**5.** Athlete in the N.B.A.'s Southwest Div

**6.** Ancient Syria

**7.** A Sinatra

**8.** Acting the bigot

**9.** Cavity fillers

**10.** Anthem's second word

**11.** Warehouse worker

**12.** Comedy's Kaplan or baseball's Kapler

**13.** Ark numbers

**18.** Area of authority

**22.** App avatars

**24.** Bit of bucolic verse

**26.** Indonesian island group

**28.** A, in Andalusia

**29.** Accomplishes perfectly, as a dismount

**30.** Asia's ___ Darya River

**31.** A point of writing

**34.** A fraction of some plays

**35.** Exasperated cry

**36.** Tries to be like

**37.** Certain Indian royalty

**39.** Adderley of bop

**40.** 'Aeneid,' e.g.

**43.** Abbr. by a golf tee

**45.** 'Cheers!,' in Berlin

**47.** Adjective for Cain

**48.** Artifacts used in teaching

**49.** Angora fabric

**50.** Big step

**53.** Extremely, in slang

**54.** Auto with a 'horse collar' grille

**55.** Asian legumes

**56.** Bread that might accompany kheer

**58.** Bad-mouth, in Britain

**59.** Aid in gaining an edge

**62.** Chairman Arafat

**63.** Amount of cash

# No. 8

## Across

1. Asian gambling destination
6. Caribbean taro
10. Army locale
14. Babe in the woods
15. Drove diagonally
16. Austrian Expressionist Schiele
17. Upright basketball player?
20. Artist Gerard ____ Borch
21. A corrosive
22. Area of Venice
23. Certain Black Sea dweller
26. Activist Guinier
27. Apt to induce goose bumps
32. Bank (on)
34. Absorbs, as a loss
35. When doubled, a book by Gauguin
36. Adequate, in verse
37. Dad's namesake: Abbr.
38. Binge-watch, maybe
39. 'Atlas Shrugged' author Rand
40. Air apparent?
42. Eager (to go)
44. They have an unstable nucleus
47. Cellos, violas, etc.: Abbr.
48. Out of place, in obstetric parlance
51. Elton's 'Through the Storm' duettist
54. Army E-3
55. Clandestine maritime org
56. Organisms studiers
60. Fungal spore cases
61. Danish shoe brand
62. CBer's sign-offs
63. Bits of a song refrain
64. City northwest of Soissons
65. Bad time for a procrastinator

## Down

1. Breast: Prefix
2. Appeared on stage
3. Exchange letters
4. Altar constellation
5. A single opening?
6. Gas for welders
7. Act feeblemindedly
8. 'Absolutely,' for short
9. Aromatic additive to natural gas
10. Bawl over
11. 'I got ____ ...'
12. Alphabetize
13. High-quality cannabis, in slang
18. Endocrine or pituitary
19. Audi logo quartet
24. Belch forth
25. Act immorally
26. Ananias, famously
28. Indie rock band Yo La ____
29. Unwilling
30. Bright moment
31. Association of criminals
32. Alternative to "honey" or "sugar"
33. 'A Day Without Rain' artist
37. British singer Stone
38. After-dinner sandwich?
40. Bantu language group
41. Airport city near Montreal
42. Boxer Graziano, formally
43. A quick study
45. Montezuma and others
46. Cookware coating
49. IV component
50. Two-time Grammy winner Houston
51. Activist ____ Alamuddin Clooney
52. Laughter, in La Mancha
53. Book after Prov.
54. A little in Spain
57. Ancient royal
58. Acquired
59. Literature Nobelist Andric

# No. 9

## Across

**1.** A fish ... or to cook it, in a way
**5.** 'Chances Are' crooner Johnny
**11.** Abbr. before Friday
**14.** Physics Nobelist Isidor
**15.** Actress DeBose
**16.** Choice marble
**17.** How many practice religion
**19.** Abbr. after a price in a Craigslist ad
**20.** Any "Jurassic Park" dinosaur
**21.** Daughter of Atlas
**22.** Adds cubes, e.g
**23.** Post-Taliban Afghan president
**25.** Hudson River town
**27.** Novel that focuses on character growth
**32.** Aping avian
**33.** Camus's 'Lettres à ____ Allemand'
**34.** 'Ain't She Sweet' composer Milton
**38.** Cleo of jazz
**41.** Affront
**42.** Bar soap brand
**44.** Arctic Circle inhabitant
**46.** They make loud noises during showers
**51.** Cotton thread
**52.** Act like aloe
**55.** Dress ____ (impersonate)
**57.** Bit of ginger powder
**60.** Bit, as of evidence
**61.** A good thing to get out of
**62.** Some sushi menu fish
**64.** Andre Young a.k.a. Dr. ____
**65.** Air carrier based in Seoul
**66.** Act the layabout
**67.** A tot may have a big one
**68.** Like heists and operas
**69.** Actual

## Down

**1.** Earthenware pot
**2.** 'Se ____ espanol'
**3.** Act like a sponge
**4.** Early Wagner opera
**5.** Athlete in the N.B.A.'s Southwest Div
**6.** Ancient Syria
**7.** A Sinatra
**8.** Acting the bigot
**9.** Cavity fillers
**10.** Anthem's second word
**11.** Warehouse worker
**12.** Comedy's Kaplan or baseball's Kapler
**13.** Ark numbers
**18.** Area of authority
**22.** App avatars
**24.** Bit of bucolic verse
**26.** Indonesian island group
**28.** A, in Andalusia
**29.** Accomplishes perfectly, as a dismount
**30.** Asia's ____ Darya River
**31.** A point of writing

**34.** A fraction of some plays
**35.** Exasperated cry
**36.** Tries to be like
**37.** Certain Indian royalty
**39.** Adderley of bop
**40.** 'Aeneid,' e.g.
**43.** Abbr. by a golf tee
**45.** 'Cheers!,' in Berlin
**47.** Adjective for Cain
**48.** Artifacts used in teaching
**49.** Angora fabric
**50.** Big step
**53.** Extremely, in slang
**54.** Auto with a 'horse collar' grille
**55.** Asian legumes
**56.** Bread that might accompany kheer
**58.** Bad-mouth, in Britain
**59.** Aid in gaining an edge
**62.** Chairman Arafat
**63.** Amount of cash

# No. 10

## Across

**1.** Barbecue go-with
**5.** Accident reminder
**9.** Black Sea port, new-style
**14.** Hip-hop's ___ Fiasco
**15.** Arno city
**16.** Be candid
**17.** Albertville's locale
**18.** A mile or a minute, e.g
**19.** 'A Full Moon in March' poet
**20.** Sweet frosting choice
**23.** One-named neo-soul singer
**24.** Aussie rapper ___ Azalea
**25.** Cost of maintenance
**27.** Accuse tentatively
**30.** Angle producers
**32.** Acapulco uncle
**33.** Pain along the course of a nerve
**37.** Unsentimental practicality
**41.** Italian P.M. nicknamed Divo Giulio
**42.** Abstract unit of exchange
**43.** Big cavity
**44.** Cold War epithet
**47.** Quality of a singing voice
**50.** Leaking goop
**51.** Archer's wife in 'The Maltese Falcon'
**52.** Sabatini or Vilas
**58.** African peninsula
**60.** Arrived at a heliport, say
**61.** Brain's ___ mater
**62.** Big name in the condiment business
**63.** A polar bear might be found on one
**64.** 'Meaty' author Samantha
**65.** 'A penny saved is a penny earned,' e.g
**66.** A fan (of)
**67.** It's a thing in Mexico

## Down

**1.** A flat, thick piece
**2.** A real doozie
**3.** Abbr. on a doctor's schedule
**4.** Small Scottish dog breed
**5.** Plant that gives us latex
**6.** Home of the Bengals, informally
**7.** Province of Saudi Arabia
**8.** A dime a dozen, e.g.
**9.** Four-year period between the quests for gold
**10.** Aberdeen river
**11.** Avoid doing
**12.** Biological bristles
**13.** Columnist Joseph
**21.** A snake may swallow one whole
**22.** Lorde who said 'The master's tools will never dismantle the master's house'
**26.** Artisan's furnace
**27.** Beginning for boy or girl
**28.** Ali, the ___ of God
**29.** Blaring
**30.** Airbnb payments
**31.** A3 maker
**33.** Annual sports contests, for short
**34.** Appreciates, as a joke
**35.** Author Dinesen
**36.** Alternative to Soave
**38.** Act greedily, perhaps
**39.** Assimilate, in Israel
**40.** Stephen of 'The Gifted'
**44.** Became inedible
**45.** A magazine can be found in one
**46.** Business agent
**47.** Campbell of 'Martin'
**48.** Covered in vines
**49.** Attachment to "Wrestle"
**50.** 'America's Finest News Source,' with 'The'
**53.** Captain's hook
**54.** Cockney greeting
**55.** A buck abroad
**56.** Financial wheeler-dealers, briefly
**57.** Bottled water brand from Canada
**59.** 'Brokeback Mountain' director Lee

# No. 11

## Across

**1.** A lot of beef?
**5.** Aida or Androcles
**10.** Dolphinfish, informally
**14.** Archaeological site, perhaps
**15.** Drank heavily
**16.** Ardent
**17.** Buggy field?
**19.** A perfect square
**20.** Digit
**21.** Bands' performance sheets
**23.** Apt pig Latin for 'trash'
**25.** 'Ariadne ___ Naxos'
**26.** Check a check, say
**29.** 'Independents Day' author Lou
**33.** Line of poetry
**37.** Ni ___ (Chinese greeting)
**38.** Basic skate trick
**39.** Bindle bearer
**40.** A little peculiar
**41.** Accomplisher
**42.** Copycat's activity
**44.** Audible reaction to a punch
**45.** Agave fiber
**46.** El ___ (Peruvian volcano)
**47.** Apparently is
**49.** 'A Midsummer Night's Dream' extra
**51.** Aid in tidying up the house
**56.** Congressional budget directives
**61.** Almost cylindrical
**62.** A transmitter
**63.** Stuffed tortillas
**65.** Sandy tract by the sea, to a Brit
**66.** Cathedral city of northern France
**67.** Big shark
**68.** Approached home, in a way
**69.** Multilane rte.
**70.** A follower, sometimes

## Down

**1.** 'Band of Gold' singer Payne
**2.** Large green moths
**3.** Capital of Hawaii?
**4.** Berry farm eponym
**5.** Women's robes of ancient Rome
**6.** Alternative to "U R funny!"
**7.** Blood drive spec.
**8.** Brand of spread for sandwiches and toast
**9.** Sliwinska of 'Dancing With the Stars'
**10.** Car exhaust systems components
**11.** Airport counter name
**12.** Aid for a solver
**13.** About midmonth
**18.** A gift of the Magi
**22.** Pachisi kin
**24.** Boorish blokes
**27.** Actor Willem
**28.** Got out of
**30.** Apply tissue to fresh lipstick, perhaps
**31.** Actress Jessica of 'Hitchcock'
**32.** All dried out
**33.** Bed accessory
**34.** Certain African antelope
**35.** African wading bird
**36.** Treated with disdain
**43.** Arizona county or river
**45.** Basketball Hall of Famer Dan
**48.** Event on the Bounty
**50.** Address in a Marseille monastery
**52.** Animated dog
**53.** Award, often
**54.** Obsessive anime fan
**55.** Acapulco cash
**56.** Actor George of 'CSI'
**57.** Alternative to a lutz
**58.** Certain pizza topping, slangily
**59.** First Secretary of War
**60.** Brown-and-white porgy
**64.** Adhere (to)

# No. 12

## Across

**1.** Appt. calendar notation

**4.** 'Feed ___, starve ...'

**9.** Be an utter bore?

**12.** Above water, barely

**15.** Almost any pre-1927 Hollywood production

**16.** Before adjustments, as in statistics

**17.** First name of a redheaded girl of kiddie lit

**18.** Set of characteristics resulting from genetics and environment

**20.** Alloy containing carbon

**21.** Accumulated facts, traditions or beliefs

**22.** Apt rhyme for 'constrain'

**23.** A bundle of nerves

**25.** Armless coats that may bear coats of arms

**27.** Footless

**30.** A bun may be next to a beehive here

**31.** Accord that's been taken back

**32.** Animal some believe to be the source of the unicorn myth

**34.** Behavioral sci.

**38.** Head of the class, in pioneer schools

**39.** Author Stephen Vincent ___

**41.** Asian river whose name is one letter away from an Ivy League college

**42.** Azure

**44.** Another name for pop

**45.** Birthplace of Antoine de Saint-Exupéry

**46.** Barely warm

**48.** Flatbread eaten in Armenia

**50.** Out of luck

**53.** Corn flour in Latin American cuisine

**54.** A founding member of the Avengers

**55.** Park in Queens?

**57.** Accident-prone

**61.** Tool sharpeners

**63.** Anatomical lashes

**64.** Army div

**65.** Cave man?

**66.** Altarpiece figure

**67.** Metric system letters

**68.** Atheist's lack

**69.** Animal group suffix

## Down

**1.** Aids for treasure hunters

**2.** Buckingham bubblehead

**3.** Act starstruck, say

**4.** Adequately, and then some

**5.** Alaskan salmon

**6.** Unfairly burdened

**7.** Like most royal descent

**8.** 'Confiteor ___ omnipotenti' (Latin prayer starter)

**9.** Alternative to a clothesline

**10.** Allegro

**11.** Athlete for whom a street outside Berlin's Olympiastadion is named

**13.** They offer rates for automobiles

**14.** Betty's sister on 'Ugly Betty'

**19.** Where one might go out to get a bite?

**24.** Amorphous amount

**26.** Awesome song, in modern slang

**27.** 'A Farewell to ___'

**28.** Busiest

**29.** C & W mecca, with 'the'

**30.** Assembly of church delegates

**33.** Requirement for running for political office

**35.** Cinematic sisterhood

**36.** French vineyard

**37.** 'What the ...?'

**40.** Samoa's monetary unit

**43.** Archer's bow wood

**47.** Italian beer brand

**49.** Adidas rival

**50.** Adherent of Zeno

**51.** 'I ___'

**52.** Gives deep massage therapy

**53.** Amble

**56.** Chocolate coins wrapped in gold or silver foil

**58.** Mother of Chas.

**59.** Danny formerly of "Law & Order: SVU"

**60.** 'Abyssinia'

**62.** Eventually appear

# No. 13

## Across

**1.** Czech form of the French 'Pierre'

**5.** Dwarf buffalo of Indonesia

**9.** Ad ___ (National Space Society magazine)

**14.** A succulent

**15.** Male offspring, in Munich

**16.** Andy of 'Radio Andy'

**17.** Ballpark pitchers

**20.** Banish, in a way

**21.** Horatian or Keatsian

**22.** A storm heading: Abbr.

**23.** A Gershwin

**25.** Grammar book, "Woe ___"

**26.** A pelican gulper is a type of one

**27.** They make deliveries

**33.** Alternative to Netflix

**34.** Abbr. on a cover letter

**35.** Argyle, e.g

**37.** Action at a bris

**38.** Acts the gadabout

**41.** Actress Sydelle

**43.** A brief quarrel

**45.** Avoid puddles, say

**46.** A Great Lake

**47.** Nora Ephron and Sofia Coppola, for two

**51.** Nasdaq, e.g.: Abbr

**53.** 'Uhh ...'

**54.** An end to peace?

**55.** Brother of Dori and Nori in 'The Hobbit'

**56.** Bends the truth

**58.** Dance music genre

**63.** Process associated with socialism

**66.** Actor Stanley

**67.** Agitate

**68.** Baseball great Sandberg

**69.** Alcohol in biofuel

**70.** Chef's array

**71.** Animal's home

## Down

**1.** A lap a minute, e.g.

**2.** Boring Company founder Musk

**3.** Actress Collette

**4.** Cassette recorder button abbrs

**5.** Forceful speaker

**6.** Antis' votes

**7.** Akron's home

**8.** Like certain battery ends

**9.** Flowering shrubs

**10.** Amour de ___ (self-love: Fr.)

**11.** Four times what's left?

**12.** Actress Della

**13.** A famous Adams

**18.** 'A Jew Today' author Wiesel

**19.** Decree ___ (legal term)

**24.** Arezzo's river

**27.** Amazed cries

**28.** Backside

**29.** Bit of crocheting

**30.** 'Dear Mama' rapper

**31.** Billionaire Carl

**32.** Big combo

**36.** Actor Dullea

**39.** Cut close

**40.** Perfume applications

**42.** Aix-___-Bains

**44.** Girl Scout emblem

**48.** A Walton

**49.** Locks up

**50.** Acronymic store name

**51.** Any of the Apennines

**52.** Dog covering

**57.** Bad thing to have showing

**59.** Abbr. associated with certain shortcuts

**60.** Breezy greeting

**61.** Anika ___ Rose of 'Dreamgirls'

**62.** Embarassing spelling mistake?

**64.** Causing skidding, maybe

**65.** Amsterdam of l'Océan Indien, e.g

# No. 14

## Across

1. Elaborate solo vocal composition
6. Dog tail?
10. Break a leg?
14. Port term on many stereos
15. A puck in a net
16. Two-stringed instrument
17. Like many flowers visited by bees
20. Actor Jeong of 'The Hangover'
21. Arctic diver
22. Wasn't all the same
23. Actress Kristen of the 'Twilight Saga' series
26. Closes a jacket
27. Countercharge
32. Anderson who managed Cincinnati's Big Red Machine
34. Chemical endings
35. Big bygone bird
36. Brie alternative
37. Sin reciprocal, in trig
38. Ballpark arbiters, briefly
39. Absorbed
40. 'A miss ___ good ...'
42. Endangered language of Northwest tribes
44. Hilarious ... or a hint to this puzzle's theme
47. Artless
48. Ad-libs and such
51. Having a little of this, a little of that
54. Designer Anna
55. Akkadian god of heaven
56. Rewards unduly
60. Actress Suvari
61. Mai ___ (drinks)
62. Ancient reference marks
63. Accessory for some comics
64. Director Gus Van ___
65. BIG DIPPER

## Down

1. Bags for flour
2. Surgical scraper
3. No longer charged
4. Followers of the largest denomination of Islam
5. A, B or C, often: Abbr.
6. Central American rodent that resembles a guinea pig
7. Annual journalism award, informally
8. 'A peculiar sort of a gal,' in song
9. Peridot, e.g.
10. Big media name
11. A freshman humanities course
12. Asian leader who had a Ph.D. from Princeton
13. California's Harvey ___ College
18. Defense against a thrust
19. Certain California wines
24. Are no longer
25. Bit of artillery fire
26. A new penny is mostly this
28. Argentina's all-time leading goal scorer
29. Resettled, in a way
30. Accident report?
31. Actress Niecy on the Hollywood Walk of Fame
32. Apt rhyme of 'aahs'
33. One of the Reagans
37. A little lower
38. A human arm bone
40. A patriarch of the Israelites
41. Faucets
42. A toaster might hold one
43. A sharpshooter needs a good one
45. Anagram of 'parent'
46. Least apt to betray
49. Belfry sound
50. Actress Essman of 'Curb Your Enthusiasm'
51. Absurdly easy victory
52. Affirm
53. Jets quarterback Smith
54. Alternative to 'roll the dice'
57. A remark from ewe?
58. A note on the music scale
59. Advocates' org.

# No. 15

## Across

**1.** Lao meat salad
**5.** Paternal kinsman
**11.** Abbr. on a headstone
**14.** Biblical dry measure
**15.** Elegant to the point of absurdity
**16.** Icelandic letter
**17.** Fast-paced alternative to Scrabble
**19.** A Maritime Prov
**20.** Asian palm
**21.** Major city of west-central Syria
**22.** Singer Jason
**23.** Actor Lee Browne
**25.** Allegro ___ (music direction)
**27.** Stephen King novel (with "The")
**32.** Classic supermodel
**33.** Crude abode
**34.** Ancient Hindu scripture
**38.** Accrue
**41.** Appealing
**42.** A lyric poem
**44.** A famous one is golden
**46.** It has drops and bolts
**51.** Swiss canton or its capital, old-style
**52.** Desserts at Luigi's
**55.** Abbr. at the top of a memo
**57.** Almond outline
**60.** Inexpensive fur
**61.** Game start?
**62.** Neurology, oncology, cardiology, etc.
**64.** Barley appendage
**65.** Antenna
**66.** A bit of superiority
**67.** Act as if
**68.** Articles of faith
**69.** Biblical verb with "thou"

## Down

**1.** Kind of pneumonia
**2.** Bitter Italian liqueur
**3.** Make a new home, in a way
**4.** Lorraine of "The Sopranos"
**5.** Alma-___, city where Trotsky was exiled
**6.** Artist Vincent van ___
**7.** 'A Doll's House' heroine
**8.** Cossack chief
**9.** Italian composer Albinoni
**10.** Alternative to ChapStick
**11.** Stay
**12.** A good one is often carried out
**13.** Face, in British slang
**18.** A Judd
**22.** Fast-swimming predators
**24.** Activist Gonzalez
**26.** Acad. or coll
**28.** African tuber
**29.** Bumps on trunks
**30.** Actor Harrison
**31.** Adjective for a fox
**34.** A.S.P.C.A. worker
**35.** Bk. after Galatians
**36.** Skeptic's specialty
**37.** Iran-Contra middleman Khashoggi
**39.** Ndamukong of the NFL
**40.** A three-hour movie might be described as one
**43.** Actor Harris and others
**45.** Actor Tom of 'The Girl Can't Help It'
**47.** Hitcher in a hurry
**48.** Admire greatly
**49.** Bursting with joy
**50.** Spanish fleet?
**53.** Cheryl who appeared on three Swimsuit Issue covers
**54.** Alaska on a map, sometimes
**55.** A bit cracked
**56.** Old-fashioned phone feature
**58.** Acetic or ascorbic, e.g
**59.** Ancient dynasty of northern China
**62.** Algonquian-speaking people
**63.** Artist Hirschfeld and namesakes

# No. 16

## Across

**1.** Fly swatter sound
**5.** "Atlas Shrugged" hero
**9.** Indonesian boat
**14.** 'Bite ___ tongue!'
**15.** Agricultural chemical
**16.** Former Colorado governor Roy
**17.** Do lead-in
**18.** Astronomer's find
**19.** Added bonus, metaphorically
**20.** Obsessed with oneself
**23.** German 'you'
**24.** Affirmations to captains
**25.** Danced in a 'pit'
**27.** Bit of Java programming
**30.** Battle
**32.** A way to vote
**33.** Cover-up
**37.** 'I can't find a flower for 'She loves me, she loves me not," said Tom ___
**41.** Alternative to Lycos
**42.** A.T.F. agent, e.g
**43.** Challenges for a speech therapist
**44.** Century segment
**47.** Ancient Mideast language
**50.** Actor Diggs
**51.** Astros, on scoreboards
**52.** Cookers for chickens and franks
**58.** 'Call to Greatness' author Stevenson
**60.** Ancient emblem of life
**61.** A Muppet
**62.** Baseball Hall-of-Famer Tim
**63.** Jane Fonda's role in 'Klute'
**64.** Aluminum potassium sulfate
**65.** Fragrant root used in perfumes
**66.** Adds to one's turf
**67.** Disintegrate, in a way, as cells in the body

## Down

**1.** Actor Noah of 'ER'
**2.** Author of "Ashes to Ashes"
**3.** A factory worker might make a dash for it
**4.** Fundamental, as an urge
**5.** Bird that catches fish by plunge-diving
**6.** Arnold Schwarzenegger's middle name
**7.** Abrasive soap brand
**8.** All-___ (four-wheel-drive system on old Toyotas)
**9.** Brand that treats acid reflux
**10.** 'Arabian Nights' bird
**11.** Barn-raising group
**12.** Figure skater known as 'The Golden Girl'
**13.** Advocated
**21.** A raised hand might indicate it
**22.** Andrea or Nicolò, in the music world
**26.** Common symbol in pronunciation: Var
**27.** Auel heroine
**28.** A sound from the tower
**29.** A handshake may seal it
**30.** Debt markers
**31.** A "Friends" real name
**33.** 'Ant Man and the ___'
**34.** A, in communications
**35.** Alaskan malamute's burden
**36.** Bad side of literature?
**38.** Goddess often depicted with a necklace of skulls
**39.** Birds' homes
**40.** Beat-based music
**44.** Morse code O's have three of them
**45.** A Cyclops has just one
**46.** Breakfast choice
**47.** Cadet's topper
**48.** Amish town in Kansas
**49.** Aid in drawing straight lines
**50.** Audibly disapproved
**53.** A close watch
**54.** Geisha's ornamental box
**55.** In a bad way
**56.** Ample avians
**57.** A handful of
**59.** Movie org. with the "100 Years" series

# No. 17

## Across

1. A herring
5. Ancient coins of Greece
10. "Dancing with the Stars" athlete
14. Act like a sot
15. Act the scaredy-cat
16. Aphids, to ladybugs
17. People might have personal ones for what they do
19. A British noble
20. Asian entertainer
21. Like this puzzle, we hope
23. Bleeth of 'Baywatch'
25. Animal in the genus Bos
26. Anti-dope group?
29. Alligators' homes
33. Actress Kruger and others
37. California wine, for short
38. Port near Osaka
39. Austria's capital, to Austrians
40. 'Ain't dead ___!'
41. Alone, as a female on stage
42. An anagram for "times"
44. Autumn blossom, briefly
45. Botanical nutrient conductor
46. Freshwater aquarium favorite
47. Apt rhyme for 'backspace'
49. Area for exchanging commodities
51. Greaseless
56. City in Sonoma County
61. Contacts' contact
62. A nestling hawk
63. Bile
65. Actress Amanda of 'Togetherness'
66. American ___
67. Almost any character on 'The Big Bang Theory'
68. Af-fjord-able city?
69. Blissful episode
70. "Come to the Mardi ___" (song)

## Down

1. Dramatically exaggerated
2. Bible book after Daniel
3. Closest or farthest orbit point
4. Basic religious belief
5. Anti-knock number
6. Accessory for Mae West or Miss Piggy
7. Accepts accountability for
8. Actor Jared
9. 'Are you kidding me?,' in texts
10. Anti-prohibition establishment
11. 'A History of the ___ Peoples' (Albert Hourani book)
12. Physics Nobelist Martin, discoverer of the tauon
13. Children's book illustrator Howard
18. Carpenters' levelers
22. Airport shuttles
24. Brewing agent
27. French lord
28. Avenger played by Paul Rudd
30. Cheer for the Vikings
31. A fisher may spin one
32. "Anna and the King" country
33. Agape, say
34. Andes capital
35. Chicken chow ___
36. First Italian course?
43. Agrarian concern
45. An inert gas
48. Bee or tea
50. Certain people of Rwanda
52. Animal in Poe's 'The Murders in the Rue Morgue'
53. Act opener?
54. 'Arrowsmith' wife
55. Back, front and Scotland
56. Gourd fruit
57. A sight for sore ___
58. Asian gold bar measure
59. Anthropologist Margaret
60. Ant contingent
64. Actress Gretchen

# No. 18

## Across

**1.** Rip off, informally

**4.** Cut slightly

**9.** Alternative to "Mac" or "Buster"

**12.** Agent of an uprising?

**15.** After-ski drink

**16.** Abner's adjective

**17.** Cuban hero Jose

**18.** Baseball cards, campaign buttons and such

**20.** Col. Potter of 'M*A*S*H,' to pals

**21.** A no-win situation?

**22.** Angels' dreams

**23.** Adjective in a seasonal song

**25.** Long flights

**27.** Approve of

**30.** Awful smell

**31.** Nickname of baseball's John Wesley Powell

**32.** Big season at Toys"R"Us

**34.** Box office busts

**38.** Bo-o-oring

**39.** Holy terrors

**41.** Former Chinese Communist military leader Lin ___

**42.** Annoying gossip

**44.** Big tooth

**45.** Bank on

**46.** Bed neatener

**48.** Big coffee exporter

**50.** Ivory Coast's largest city

**53.** Actor Singer

**54.** Backfire noise

**55.** Battery-powered CBD dispenser

**57.** Anne Frank's hideout

**61.** Transferable to another owner

**63.** Red of early jazz

**64.** Airport delayer

**65.** Checks figures?

**66.** A judge is one

**67.** "A Bridge ___ Far"

**68.** 'A Room With a View' clergyman

**69.** OB/___

## Down

**1.** Aerobics locales

**2.** 'Awright!'

**3.** Cut away the outer layer of

**4.** Almost boil

**5.** Baseball's Hideo

**6.** Giant glaciers

**7.** Aid for achieving a flat stomach?

**8.** Alaskan Klee ___ (small dog breed)

**9.** 'Anne Frank: The Diary of a Young Girl' audiobook narrator Selma

**10.** Kings Peak's range

**11.** Big name in American fashion design

**13.** Tool for drawing a perfect line

**14.** King of Tartary in 'Turandot'

**19.** Health professional who has your back?

**24.** Fields suitable for grazing (var.)

**26.** Big dollop

**27.** Ann's advice-giving sister

**28.** Agricultural giant with the mascot Bobby Banana

**29.** Bellyacher's sound

**30.** Baker's bagful

**33.** Like something that can't be defended

**35.** Attitude

**36.** Badly worn, as tires

**37.** Alternative milk source

**40.** Antarctic bird

**43.** Descriptive wd

**47.** Forced feeding, as with a tube

**49.** Aid package component

**50.** At the rear, to a sailor

**51.** Bear in Kipling's "The Jungle book"

**52.** Architect Jones

**53.** Attorney general before Thornburgh

**56.** Academy freshman

**58.** A lecture on it might be full of tangents

**59.** Actress Judith

**60.** Base of some ethanol

**62.** Aristocrat, in British slang

# No. 19

## Across

**1.** Uncouth Bournemouth youth
**5.** A Lennon
**9.** Conceited smile
**14.** A kid might skip it
**15.** Senator Mike from Wyoming
**16.** A bit creepy
**17.** Training times
**20.** Basque Country metropolis
**21.** Author Emile
**22.** 'Am I an idiot!'
**23.** Asian address
**25.** Boundary: Abbr.
**26.** Alfonso XIII's consort
**27.** Nurse ___ (medical workers)
**33.** Disgusted sound
**34.** Acquisition for some vacationers
**35.** A chip off the old flock?
**37.** Aluminum silicate
**38.** DTs sufferer, for short
**41.** Alternative to cedar
**43.** Penta- doubled
**45.** Beach bird
**46.** Acad
**47.** Reporters who were trained in Washington, D.C.?
**51.** Commonly
**53.** Almost worthless money
**54.** 'A cockroach!'
**55.** Actress Arthur
**56.** Actress Fisher
**58.** Ancient Greek region
**63.** Presidential appointments
**66.** Acquire by fraud
**67.** 'Corydon' author
**68.** A Scottish loch
**69.** Access All ___ (words on a pass)
**70.** An avocado pit is one
**71.** Appliance at a bakery

## Down

**1.** Ariel's friend Sebastian, e.g
**2.** A Pueblo Indian
**3.** G.E. product: Abbr.
**4.** Action word
**5.** Havana lass
**6.** Adenoidectomy specialist, for short
**7.** Actor Ansari
**8.** One of the Amati family of violin makers
**9.** Bagel choices
**10.** 'Big whoop'
**11.** Like mother-of-pearl
**12.** Harass and insult, slangily
**13.** Gaga contemporary
**18.** A cardinal point
**19.** Tiger Woods's ex
**24.** A title might be presented in it: Abbr
**27.** Barbara who wrote 'Quartet in Autumn'
**28.** Actor Tim of "WKRP in Cincinnati"
**29.** O.K.
**30.** New Mexico's ___ Canyon, a national historic park site
**31.** Aide for a cartoonist
**32.** Anatomical networks
**36.** Charge a criminal?
**39.** 'Deus ___' (1976 sci-fi novel)
**40.** Caused admiration
**42.** Diamond wts
**44.** Baseball or basketball statistics
**48.** Attempt at a carnival booth
**49.** Labor camps
**50.** 'Aloha Oe' accompaniers
**51.** 'A Promised Land' memoirist
**52.** Big bone
**57.** As straight as ___
**59.** 'Ack!'
**60.** Actor Schreiber
**61.** Alter ___ amicus
**62.** A.A.A. member?: Abbr.
**64.** BHO's signature legislation
**65.** A famous one begins 'How sleep the brave ...'

# No. 20

## Across

**1.** Basil and pine-nuts sauce
**6.** Architect ___ Gilbert
**10.** A 'Bonanza' brother
**14.** Pis ___ (the last resort)
**15.** All-grade
**16.** Actor and tap dancer Hill
**17.** Amounts owed at a diner?
**20.** Academia figure
**21.** Earliest recorded Chinese dynasty
**22.** Coffee ___ (social gathering)
**23.** Assigns new actors
**26.** Abstract artist Mondrian
**27.** Gates and Jobs, e.g.
**32.** Asian shrine
**34.** Arthurian days, e.g
**35.** As matters stand
**36.** Port on the Firth of Lorne
**37.** Captors of Patty Hearst: Abbr.
**38.** Animal whose young is a calf
**39.** ABC or Fox, in Variety-speak
**40.** A law ___ itself
**42.** G. P. ___ (early book publisher)
**44.** Helped someone move into an office, say
**47.** A leg up
**48.** Augmented fourth
**51.** Becomes liable for
**54.** Aromatic Asian soup
**55.** Big chunk of Eur.
**56.** Experts on the brain
**60.** Actress Diane of 'Numb3rs'
**61.** Baseball analyst Hershiser
**62.** Beyond beefy
**63.** Church calendar
**64.** Acknowledgments
**65.** French artist Odilon ___

## Down

**1.** An Indiana NBA player
**2.** Act impulsively, as young lovers
**3.** Water flow regulator
**4.** A fourth of what's left?
**5.** Bit for the barker
**6.** Bright red
**7.** Actress Jessica
**8.** Al Green song '___-La-La'
**9.** Comparatively luxurious
**10.** Grown together, in biology
**11.** Air carrier
**12.** A Baldwin bro
**13.** Barrier against burrowers
**18.** A face in the crowd?
**19.** Coeur d' ___, Idaho
**24.** Abbr. in a book of quotations
**25.** Abbr. after 'Rev.' or before 'dev.'
**26.** Indonesian outrigger
**28.** Air race marker
**29.** Not yet ready to be deposited
**30.** Catholic ecclesiastical court
**31.** Began a triathlon
**32.** American Indian cornbread
**33.** A son of Adam
**37.** Anagram of 'pots'
**38.** Alteration canceler
**40.** Developing, after "in"
**41.** Swedish soprano noted for her Wagnerian roles
**42.** Advocate of 'justicialismo'
**43.** Alleged mentalist Geller
**45.** Deep-fried Mexican treat
**46.** A Rosenberg and others
**49.** Completely preposterous
**50.** Bad ___ (Lower Saxony city)
**51.** Brochure's contents
**52.** A few feet away
**53.** Bean ___
**54.** Blotchy
**57.** Balkan land, in the Olympics
**58.** A.L. East squad
**59.** 'Can ___ dreaming?'

# No. 21

## Across

**1.** Animal's nail
**5.** Crown covers
**11.** A TD is worth six: Abbr.
**14.** Feature of 'pasta' and 'basta'
**15.** Gluten-free Japanese soy sauce
**16.** Activist Aruna
**17.** Swearing-in figure
**19.** Ancient times, in ancient times
**20.** Appreciation
**21.** Afternoon TV's Dr. ___
**22.** Bygone French coins
**23.** West Sumatra's capital
**25.** Aristocrat
**27.** Carfax report?
**32.** Coal area
**33.** An ex of Ava
**34.** Coffee cup holder
**38.** Doublets
**41.** Author of 'Chaim Lederer's Return'
**42.** Director Kurosawa
**44.** Ugly ones
**46.** Incredible stretch of asphalt
**51.** Oscar-winning director of 'My Fair Lady'
**52.** Assuaging agents
**55.** Alligator logo brand, once
**57.** Chops (off)
**60.** Alfred of I.Q. testing
**61.** Adriatique ou Baltique
**62.** Wrongdoing
**64.** A hand
**65.** All ready for final assembly
**66.** "Can I ___ witness?"
**67.** Appalachians, e.g.: Abbr.
**68.** Intestinal opening?
**69.** Baseball's "Blue Moon"

## Down

**1.** Adjective for cool weather
**2.** First blank on a form
**3.** Actress Blake
**4.** Onetime Wisconsin-based insurance giant
**5.** Actor/comic Gilliam
**6.** A fish that nags?
**7.** Asian au pair
**8.** Bilingual American, often
**9.** Computer language that sounds like a literary intro
**10.** 'Aaron Burr, ___'
**11.** Rules of conduct
**12.** Cough-syrup ingredient
**13.** Barrett and Hoff
**18.** Bathroom door sign
**22.** One of Jupiter's moons
**24.** Cattle drive tool
**26.** A couple of cups?
**28.** American Pharoah or Citation
**29.** About to blow
**30.** Andy Capp's comment
**31.** Mumbled assent
**34.** Some pepperoni orders, informally
**35.** When doubled, a Thor Heyerdahl book
**36.** Fall openers
**37.** 'Civilization and Its Discontents' author
**39.** A deer, a female deer
**40.** Band with the debut album 'Diamond Life'
**43.** Ancient animal shelter
**45.** At-home test kit components
**47.** Toyota Camry model
**48.** Class of '1984'
**49.** Alternative to Parmesan
**50.** Felt a longing
**53.** Book's right-hand page
**54.** Antique engine's power source
**55.** Certain congregation leader
**56.** Time, in Germany
**58.** 'All gone!'
**59.** Affix a brand on
**62.** Abbr. in a car review
**63.** Actress Olivia d'___

## Across

**1.** Ball of thread
**5.** Costa ___
**9.** Angels slugger Justin
**14.** Beatle George studied under him
**15.** Admits (to)
**16.** English Channel borough
**17.** A brother of Donald Jr
**18.** Activity in a dohyo
**19.** B in music?
**20.** Rehearsal
**23.** Afflict
**24.** Actor Bremner of 'Wonder Woman'
**25.** Biblical matriarch
**27.** Hostage holder
**30.** Bagpipe sound
**32.** Commercial lead-in to Clean
**33.** Rebels
**37.** Activity for a nitpicking boss
**41.** One who's not being precise
**42.** A word before you go
**43.** Bishop's deputy
**44.** Award
**47.** Address the flock
**50.** Baby ___ (salad ingredient)
**51.** Ancient law
**52.** Remindful
**58.** Firenze friend
**60.** Amway competitor
**61.** Accurate, as aim
**62.** Aquiline weapon
**63.** Actor Chad or Rob
**64.** Adjective after "ye"
**65.** Accepts customers
**66.** Airborne fish eaters
**67.** Accordion component

## Down

**1.** All aboard?
**2.** Actress ___ Flynn Boyle
**3.** Adjective that describes It
**4.** Small gate
**5.** Bacon amount
**6.** Bury in a vase
**7.** Bit of hunting gear, for short
**8.** Baseball brother
**9.** Additional payment
**10.** Bluegrass genus
**11.** Ark contents
**12.** Almost any doo-wop song
**13.** 'Jurassic Park' co-star Sam
**21.** A couple
**22.** Composer born in Bergen
**26.** Animal metaphor for a quiet person
**27.** Accept an invitation, say
**28.** About which the Earth turns
**29.** Ancient Brit
**30.** Acapulco address
**31.** A knot or burl in wood
**33.** Couple of words before "tat"
**34.** Amount in an i.o.u
**35.** Greek goddess of war
**36.** Anxiously worry
**38.** Kentucky Derby winner ___ Ridge
**39.** O's overseas
**40.** Papier-___
**44.** Fitzgerald-Milhous go-between
**45.** A couple of dollars?
**46.** Any slice of pizza, geometrically
**47.** Academy founder
**48.** Alter, as a site layout
**49.** Banish
**50.** Familiar
**53.** Androgen producer
**54.** Actor and songwriter Novello
**55.** Agatha contemporary
**56.** Acrylic nail shade
**57.** Angry (with "off")
**59.** Anti body?

# No. 23

## Across

**1.** Action to a newborn baby's bottom
**5.** Frequent host town of the British Open
**10.** Highly contagious resp. illness
**14.** A ditz hasn't one
**15.** Agave root
**16.** Those, to Robert Burns
**17.** Actor whose character is stung in 'The Sting'
**19.** Accompaniment at an Indian restaurant
**20.** Early computer forum
**21.** Course of study
**23.** Soprano Josephine
**25.** Annoying bark
**26.** Animal also known as a hog-nosed coon
**29.** Conceal, in a way
**33.** Apply carelessly
**37.** Afrique du ___
**38.** San Francisco Bay's ___ Buena Island
**39.** A witch's nose might have one
**40.** Lull ending
**41.** Foretell the future
**42.** Revoke, as a will
**44.** Account amt.
**45.** Actor Davis
**46.** Bullfight procession
**47.** Banished to Elba
**49.** Bath tissue feature
**51.** Asparagus unit
**56.** Apparition
**61.** In music, a full interval higher or lower than written
**62.** A bit more than a trot
**63.** Evidence that's no longer in circulation?
**65.** Animals hidden backward in 'cheese wedge'
**66.** Delta ___ of "Designing Women"
**67.** Bon Jovi's 'You Give Love ___ Name'
**68.** Boomers' followers
**69.** A bit off
**70.** Asian princess

## Down

**1.** Abort, as a mission
**2.** Author Mario Vargas ___
**3.** French operatic composer
**4.** Hammer ends
**5.** Angel on one's shoulder, say
**6.** Abbr. in an apt. ad
**7.** Aahs' kin
**8.** Antiaging cream brand
**9.** As of late
**10.** Like some gowns
**11.** 'A grand, ungodly, godlike man' in fiction
**12.** Alfredo sauce brand
**13.** A proverbial seven
**18.** Heave
**22.** Delicate, in a way
**24.** Coating for roasted peas
**27.** Bass brass
**28.** Pastoral compositions
**30.** Battle of Helm's Deep force
**31.** Archaeological shelter
**32.** 'American Pie' actor Eddie ___ Thomas
**33.** Barter
**34.** Russian auto make
**35.** An anagram for "rose"
**36.** Cliff consideration
**43.** Birds and snakes do it
**45.** American playwright
**48.** Lyric poems
**50.** Start of a cartoon cry
**52.** Certain perfume
**53.** Most sacred building in Islam
**54.** Alternative to Dasani or Deer Park
**55.** Actress Oakes of 'CHiPs'
**56.** Common movie house name ending
**57.** British commander at Bunker Hill
**58.** Charades player, at times
**59.** Area of poverty
**60.** Memento ___
**64.** Approves, briefly

# No. 24

## Across

1. O.T. book
4. Bit for Fido, perhaps
9. Old phone trio
12. 'A Dog of Flanders' author
15. Baja breakfast order
16. 'A likely story!'
17. Big name in fishing gear
18. Like Ahab's pursuit of Moby Dick
20. Accordion bellows feature
21. Amorous cartoon skunk
22. Accepted a lesser charge, say
23. Baldies' envy
25. Cool with what others are doing
27. Actor O'Brien
30. Company indicator?
31. Basketball star Williamson
32. Elves, in poetry
34. The appendix extends from it
38. Abbr. after old generals' names
39. Cast about
41. Daughter of Katie Holmes and Tom Cruise
42. 'Being There' director
44. Addams Family nickname
45. Big name in tennis balls
46. Actor Murphy of old westerns
48. Ancient Macedonian capital
50. Dense grove
53. Fort ___ (Arlington army post)
54. Alternative to rap and R&B
55. Add salt to, maybe
57. Area of India
61. First Kentucky Derby winner
63. All but the signal, in radio
64. Commercial lead-in to mart
65. Bits of créativité
66. Bandleader Skinnay
67. ESPN broadcaster Bob
68. Annoying, as a gnat
69. Guys' dates, informally

## Down

1. Alternative to a condo
2. Be a pitcher
3. Bank of France?
4. Bakery and pharmacy
5. Aptly named Nissan
6. What a mail order merchant wants
7. Brand advertised by Jennifer Aniston
8. Blood-type abbr.
9. Temple U. setting
10. Dancer with glowsticks, often
11. Chicago's ___ Aquarium
13. Card player's favorite baseball team?
14. Fancy car starter?
19. Bicycle mechanic?
24. Acrobat displays
26. Abbr. at the top of an email
27. Alternative rock's Better Than ___
28. Ceases to live
29. Army worm, eventually
30. Mr. Mister song named after a prayer
33. Mindsets
35. Aids after blanking out
36. Ash cans?
37. 'Dracula' girl
40. Byproduct of cheesemaking
43. Chortle
47. Adjudicate
49. American representative to France during the Revolutionary War
50. Cast a wide net
51. Goddesses guarding the gates of Olympus
52. How to respond to an affront
53. Chaotic, as a situation
56. Assault the nostrils
58. Act as informer
59. 'A likely story'
60. A finger painter may make one
62. A cash one is generally preferred

# No. 25

## Across

1. Bridal gown designer Di Santo
5. Asian flatbread
9. Creature that can lick its own eyes
14. Japanese hot pot
15. Anagram of "lies"
16. Actress Massey
17. Honest sort
20. Accompanier of a harrow, in Harrow
21. Add evenly, as cream or sugar
22. A driver may hit it
23. Abbr. for Lucasfilm
25. A bit of a joule
26. Aged
27. LSD can cause it
33. Avis features
34. Academy Award winner for 'Moonlight' and 'Green Book'
35. Eight, as a prefix
37. Animal rights org
38. Animation studio with a lamp mascot
41. 'Daktari' actor Rhodes
43. Adam's apple locale
45. A camel may be executed on it
46. Director Johnson
47. Lester bats while ...
51. A Thai language
53. "Am ___ believe . . ."
54. A for Adenauer
55. 'Er-r ...'
56. Accessory for a Brownie
58. Japanese market index
63. Within a key TV demographic
66. Agra attire (Var.)
67. Always
68. Actor Ray
69. Bandleader called 'The Ol' Perfessor'
70. Investigators: Abbr.
71. Ornament that may be worn with sandals

## Down

1. Clouseau title: Abbr.
2. Countrywide: Abbr
3. Aragon bisector
4. All-Pro linebacker Junior of the Chargers
5. Bedtime drink
6. A grate build-up
7. Climbing figs
8. Arizona alternative
9. Armani with a plaque on the Rodeo Drive Walk of Style
10. 'A New World Record' grp.
11. White-scutted creature
12. Bow's cousin
13. Did crew work
18. Eskimo home: Var
19. Al who performed the theme for "The Green Hornet"
24. Capital and largest city of East Timor
27. Accident
28. Architect William Van ___
29. Annoying folks at the theater
30. Archibald ___ (Cary Grant's real name)
31. Undeliverable letter, to a postal worker
32. Adobe color
36. Romanian city on the Mures
39. A little of a large lot?
40. Employees in the sugar industry
42. Aetna's bus.
44. Tush
48. A judge might issue one
49. Chucked
50. Alive, competitively
51. Ukrainian city
52. Brand name that's pig Latin for a band name
57. Hauled on board
59. Euphoric leaf
60. About two lbs
61. Author of "The Neverending Story"
62. Aircraft designer Sikorsky
64. Adjective between a pair of surnames
65. Achieved, as a sales quota

# No. 26

## Across

**1.** Large, pale antelope
**6.** Badgered
**10.** Artist given the derisive nickname 'Avida Dollars,' an anagram of his full name
**14.** Actor born Laszlo Loewenstein
**15.** A social sci.
**16.** Aesir leader
**17.** Off-putting?
**20.** Akihito's title: Abbr
**21.** Aristotle character
**22.** Almost too much
**23.** Composer Antonio
**26.** American Theatre Wing award
**27.** CAPITAL ONE/SUN merger with a succinct press release
**32.** GRUMPY
**34.** A group of them is called un archipel
**35.** Aberdeen denial
**36.** Accelerates sharply
**37.** A.C. letters
**38.** Helping hound
**39.** 'A Chorus Line' number
**40.** Chinese dynasty before the Shang
**42.** Tear off forcefully
**44.** Spy who works for a Washington paper?
**47.** Act ___ impulse
**48.** Nine-sided figure
**51.** Battle-ready mounts
**54.** Actor Alastair
**55.** Add-on for Gator
**56.** Like some officers
**60.** Apex predator in all of the world's oceans
**61.** A dog's age
**62.** Largest steel producer in the U.S
**63.** A sudden, short breath
**64.** Courtesy title overseas
**65.** Action locus

## Down

**1.** French peaks
**2.** Puccini's 'Nessun ___'
**3.** Hinged sections on some dining tables
**4.** A compass can help you make one
**5.** Ballot marker
**6.** Forward, as a package
**7.** Arachnid-appropriate prefix
**8.** "And how!"
**9.** Bestow with a title
**10.** Certain domain suffix
**11.** Sarah McLachlan hit
**12.** Absorbent cotton
**13.** 'A Loss of Roses' playwright
**18.** An orderly grouping
**19.** Andrea Bocelli deliveries
**24.** Airbnb alternatives
**25.** Johann ___, opponent of Martin Luther
**26.** Finnish city near the Arctic Circle
**28.** Bad member to pick?
**29.** Lack of polish
**30.** Argo's array
**31.** Actress Campbell
**32.** Alfalfa or buckwheat
**33.** A place to play keno
**37.** Adverb in both French and Spanish
**38.** Capital on the island of Viti Levu
**40.** John Wayne film based on a Louis L'Amour story
**41.** Suffered from cramps, say
**42.** Bitty bits
**43.** Actor Diesel
**45.** Boot feature
**46.** Child actress Jones of 'Family Affair'
**49.** Ancient arts venue
**50.** Actress Volz
**51.** Be amorous with, in Britain
**52.** Japanese code word meaning 'tiger'
**53.** Abbr. at the bottom of a business letter
**54.** Ireland's ___ Féin
**57.** Angus beef?
**58.** All ___ day's work
**59.** Belonging to us

# No. 27

## Across

**1.** Controversial sunscreen ingredient
**5.** A passenger on
**11.** Spanish author Baroja y Nessi
**14.** 'Being ___' (2015 documentary featuring many wipeouts)
**15.** Beat poet?
**16.** Apt name for a thief
**17.** Writing done GRAPHICALLY
**19.** Battle of ___ Jima
**20.** Cardigans, e.g.
**21.** Cheese type
**22.** Animal balancing a beachball on its nose
**23.** Addison's co-author
**25.** Author Nin
**27.** Astounded by how much weight you've gained?
**32.** Arc on a music score
**33.** Bounce back, as stock prices
**34.** Amer. ally in W.W. II
**38.** Ban's predecessor at the U.N.
**41.** Actor-singer Lovett
**42.** Dreidel letter
**44.** Antiquated interjection
**46.** Native name for the Iroquois Confederacy
**51.** Los ___, Calif.
**52.** Earthling, in sci-fi
**55.** Accept a contract
**57.** Arboreal monkey
**60.** Ceska Republika capital
**61.** Drink for Hercule Poirot
**62.** Shortens a sentence, say
**64.** Ashram sounds
**65.** Indolent
**66.** A kid drinks from one
**67.** Angkor ___
**68.** Gunsmith with Smith
**69.** American Girl doll with a back story on the Underground Railroad

## Down

**1.** Apple quantities
**2.** Before, in Burgundy
**3.** Agnostic's lack
**4.** Mobile phone company
**5.** Birthplace of the tango: Abbr
**6.** Arrowhead feature
**7.** A gem of a lady?
**8.** Be published
**9.** Arranged anew, as paintings
**10.** Alcohol-free
**11.** Like some robes
**12.** A Siouan
**13.** Ancient Greek coin
**18.** Cozumel y Mallorca, por ejemplo
**22.** Agave fiber used in rugs
**24.** Ancient city with remains near Aleppo
**26.** Alpine river
**28.** Ballerina's hairdo
**29.** Birds by sea cliffs
**30.** Addition, in construction
**31.** Add color to
**34.** An expression of disdain
**35.** Adelaide-born pop singer
**36.** Most self-satisfied
**37.** Form of fortification
**39.** A leader no matter how you look at it
**40.** Kind of mile: Abbr
**43.** Abate, with 'up'
**45.** Smolensk's river
**47.** Add an explanation to
**48.** Brother and husband of Isis
**49.** Annoyances for readers
**50.** Blank, now
**53.** A good way to leave Vegas
**54.** Bad-tasting, maybe
**55.** Barge
**56.** Advice columnist Kurtz
**58.** Art colony in New Mexico
**59.** Itself: Lat
**62.** 'BAM!' relative
**63.** Adult female chicken

# No. 28

## Across

**1.** Actor Max of "The Beverly Hillbillies"
**5.** Amusement ___
**9.** Baseball bobbles
**14.** Actress Kedrova
**15.** Anita of jazz
**16.** Baseball's Chase
**17.** 'A Prayer for ___ Meany'
**18.** Almond ___ (candy brand)
**19.** Kind of terrier
**20.** 'Chiropractor heads into the ___!'
**23.** A touching game
**24.** Allocation of some pork spending?
**25.** Brawl in the backwoods
**27.** Acropolis figure
**30.** 'Yuck!!'
**32.** Indian novelist Raja ___
**33.** One not to beat
**37.** Bug elimination
**41.** Art expert, at times
**42.** Bemoans
**43.** A Parisian's right?
**44.** Tarantino title character
**47.** Car made in Spring Hill, Tenn.
**50.** A new one is nearly invisible
**51.** Brew from Washington State, familiarly
**52.** Proven
**58.** Cézanne colleague
**60.** Alter ___ (another exactly the same)
**61.** 'Dang, that's cool'
**62.** About
**63.** A 'hot' one is controversial
**64.** Actress Lanchester
**65.** Badminton opener
**66.** A stake, metaphorically
**67.** Cambodian bread

## Down

**1.** Amoeba, e.g
**2.** Audio equipment brand
**3.** A util
**4.** Cause irritation
**5.** Balthasar's true identity, in Shakespeare
**6.** Accessorize
**7.** A long one may have legs
**8.** Basic monetary unit in Myanmar
**9.** Hombre-to-be
**10.** Acting expert Hagen
**11.** Darts
**12.** Far from domesticated
**13.** J. M. ___, 'The Playboy of the Western World' playwright
**21.** Abel, to Adam
**22.** Belief
**26.** Amount in a whiskey glass
**27.** 'Thou ___ lady': King Lear
**28.** Ball field covering
**29.** A circus lion may jump through one
**30.** Assail
**31.** Actor Bert
**33.** Actor Arnaz of 'I Love Lucy'
**34.** Artist Rembrandt van ___
**35.** A bit tight
**36.** Big breakfast brand
**38.** A language of Pakistan
**39.** Hair piece?
**40.** Animals depicted on the Ishtar Gate
**44.** Stone arrangement, like Stonehenge
**45.** Lansing of "Love That Bob"
**46.** Cheater's peeked-at item
**47.** Bodies of organisms
**48.** 'A Night at the Opera' tune
**49.** Jazz pianist McCoy ___
**50.** Mandela's presidential successor
**53.** Chickadees' kin
**54.** Alaskan island or its principal town
**55.** Colorful Hindu festival
**56.** Abate
**57.** Indian dish made with stewed legumes
**59.** Card holder: Abbr

# No. 29

## Across

**1.** Coll. periods
**5.** An edict of the Russian tsar
**10.** A distant point
**14.** Alternative to a staple
**15.** Arid region of Israel
**16.** A stud may hang around here
**17.** Payment sent
**19.** Auto garage service
**20.** Actor Don
**21.** Beersheba citizens
**23.** Around June or July
**25.** Compliment to a chef
**26.** Canadian catch
**29.** Artist Frida
**33.** Card game of Spanish origin
**37.** A.T.M. expense
**38.** Golfer Ed
**39.** Comedian "Colonel Maggie" Martha
**40.** Audible pauses
**41.** 'Affirmative, ___, I read you' (line in '2001: A Space Odyssey')
**42.** Activist Thunberg
**44.** Astronaut Grissom
**45.** Hindu scriptures
**46.** Breakfast table staple: Var.
**47.** Activist Garner
**49.** Abbr. for Jesse Jackson
**51.** Have a healthy diet
**56.** It crosses the nave
**61.** Hardly like a he-man
**62.** American patriot Nathan
**63.** Vets, once
**65.** Agency that tracks Carmen Sandiego
**66.** Act the coxcomb
**67.** Baja California resort
**68.** Certain thick-piled rugs
**69.** Amid
**70.** Construction toy brand

## Down

**1.** Bug out
**2.** Certain resin
**3.** Acted out
**4.** Hot, food-wise
**5.** Int'l org. of inspectors
**6.** Brownish-green parrot
**7.** Hindu god of fire
**8.** Abbreviated moments
**9.** All possible
**10.** Baroque dance form
**11.** Ball for the fans
**12.** 'Broad City' actress Jacobson
**13.** Actor Roger
**18.** Benny Goodman's '___ Foolish Things'
**22.** Birds with coastal colonies
**24.** Haven, as for endangered wildlife
**27.** Animal in "Madagascar"
**28.** Actress O'Shea
**30.** Amount of cabbage
**31.** Bulgarian coins
**32.** Adoring poems
**33.** A.A. and A.A.A.
**34.** Activist Copeny
**35.** 'Why Won't You Date Me?' host Nicole
**36.** Soldiers home from service, e.g.
**43.** Animals of the species Pan troglodyte
**45.** Oracular
**48.** Capturing
**50.** Big name in motor scooters
**52.** Sunken ship
**53.** Heifetz contemporary
**54.** 'Ich ___ dich' (German words of endearment)
**55.** Big name in bone china
**56.** Dialectal direction
**57.** A bit blue
**58.** Author ___ Luz Villanueva
**59.** A cold wave can produce one
**60.** BlackBerry rival
**64.** Title for one on the way to sainthood: Abbr.

# No. 30

## Across

1. 'Another thing . . .' in a text
4. Arboretum growth
9. Alien from Melmac
12. Coral areas
15. Actress Téa
16. Act lovey-dovey
17. Anticipate
18. Home of the Cowboys' stadium
20. Greek New Age musician
21. Gamer's "Yay!"
22. Aid for a shopper
23. Birthstones, e.g
25. Fillets
27. City on Lake Ontario
30. Do new voice-overs
31. Donald of the Major League Baseball Players Association
32. Alternative to MasterCard and Visa, informally
34. People with safe jobs?
38. Angel's nightmare
39. Breaks at the ranch
41. Bad thing to drop in public
42. Reference section staple
44. Buttocks, in slang
45. Barbecue dish
46. Metrical accent
48. A perfect place
50. Ad supplier
53. Advice from Weight Watchers
54. Abrupt ending of a sort
55. Caster of spells
57. Bathroom division
61. Arkansas, Pennsylvania, Ohio
63. Comic attachment?
64. N.B.A. scoring stat
65. Babies' places
66. Old Russian co-op
67. A pittance, slangily
68. Attendance count
69. Actor Brynner

## Down

1. Act like a jackass
2. Esther Martinez's language
3. Accustom to solid food, e.g.
4. Barbecue sides
5. Achilles or Ajax
6. Obsolescent desktop accessories
7. 'It's time to fly' advertiser
8. Bargain basement container
9. Be a cast member of
10. Baggy
11. Abundant sources
13. Hands-on art medium
14. Author Larsson
19. Basketball showman
24. A drawbridge may span it
26. Act like a bull?
27. Easy as falling ___ log
28. Abandon a position
29. 'For ___ the Bell Tolls'
30. Br'er Rabbit storyteller
33. Ripens
35. Basic of golf instruction
36. Aloo ___
37. City rebuilt by Darius I
40. Chinese for 'water'
43. Adds as an additional recipient, in email
47. Beefsteak or cherry
49. Actress Allen
50. Bacterial infection, for short
51. Browning title character
52. Any science, loosely
53. Arnaz, Sr. and Jr
56. Actor Richard of 'Chicago'
58. A bit pretentious
59. In ___ of (replacing)
60. Act indolent
62. A large cask

# No. 31

## Across

**1.** Color of a Sonora sunset, perhaps
**5.** Audi rival
**9.** Compound added to natural gas to give it an odor
**14.** A billion years
**15.** 'Able was I ere I saw ___'
**16.** A couple of octaves, for most singers
**17.** In a hilarious manner
**20.** Actress Cuthbert of '24'
**21.** Any of three O.K. Corral figures
**22.** Abbr. after a colonel's name, maybe
**23.** 'A little ___ the mightiest Julius fell': Shak.
**25.** A place to go in London?
**26.** Central Dutch city
**27.** Tolerant of other opinions
**33.** Aliases, informally
**34.** Cal. col. heading
**35.** Je ne ___ quoi
**37.** Ambulance's destination: Abbr
**38.** Author Canetti
**41.** A runner may enter one
**43.** Converts to a cause, briefly
**45.** Addis Ababa is its cap.
**46.** 'A kind of praise': John Gay
**47.** Scream elicitor
**51.** Antique coin
**53.** A driver might dip into it
**54.** 'A Room of One's ___'
**55.** A.T.M. need
**56.** Certain YouTube posting
**58.** 'Academica' author
**63.** Hypes
**66.** Big name in vacuum cleaners
**67.** Former French coins
**68.** Actress and former mixed martial arts champion Carano
**69.** Nostril
**70.** Actress Falco
**71.** Ascend dramatically

## Down

**1.** Demolish, British-style
**2.** Aix eye
**3.** 'Harvesting the Heart' author Picoult
**4.** A good deal of binary code
**5.** Bust up
**6.** Accompanier of "thumbs" and "ears"
**7.** Anne Nichols title hero
**8.** One of the Iron Chefs on 'Iron Chef America'
**9.** Camera stabilizers
**10.** Ben Solo's father
**11.** Food label listing
**12.** Behaved creepily, in a way
**13.** MacArthur victory site
**18.** 'Fer ___!'
**19.** Arcade game based on a film of the same name
**24.** A month in Tel Aviv
**27.** Di-dah lead-in
**28.** Big name in copiers
**29.** One always hoping to score
**30.** City on the Gulf of Finland
**31.** Getty Center architect Richard
**32.** Chair designer Charles
**36.** Ballesteros of golf
**39.** Bobby Darin's record label
**40.** Cabinet for displaying wares
**42.** Mars : Roman :: ___ : Norse
**44.** Czech neighbors
**48.** Airy melody
**49.** Ava's role in 'Mogambo'
**50.** Blue dye
**51.** Big ink purveyor
**52.** Former Olds Cutlass
**57.** B or B+, say
**59.** Camels, e.g., for short
**60.** Basso Pinza
**61.** Actress Sofer
**62.** Gravel ridges
**64.** A high school dept.
**65.** Air Tahiti ___ (carrier to Papeete)

# No. 32

## Across

**1.** Alamo assault
**6.** Andy of old comics
**10.** Bit of viral web content
**14.** Beauty product
**15.** A gold one might be given for a job well done
**16.** Doctor and writer Gawande
**17.** Some expressions of false humility
**20.** Actress Long
**21.** A dance step
**22.** Ancient Roman council
**23.** Drink made with red wine and fruit
**26.** Baseball star in Senate steroid hearings
**27.** Negotiators who are mostly talk
**32.** Does a bakery job
**34.** Au pair's charge
**35.** Alt's opposite
**36.** Actor Calhoun
**37.** Disease preventer, in slang
**38.** A type of arch
**39.** A heavy metal band may have it
**40.** Amazon category
**42.** Bar fights?
**44.** Modulating between dialects
**47.** Capital of Shaanxi province
**48.** Most angular
**51.** Certain poplars
**54.** A really good place to sit?
**55.** Abba's 'Mamma ___'
**56.** Inconsideration
**60.** Between a rock and a hard place
**61.** 'Aeneid' figure
**62.** A liar's are "on fire"
**63.** Granite paving block
**64.** A or B, on an LP
**65.** Architectural features of Greco-Roman temples

## Down

**1.** Cold-cocks
**2.** Aegean region
**3.** Like some species
**4.** 'Ain't that something!'
**5.** Accidentally hit 'Reply All,' say
**6.** Swiss resort popular with jet-setters
**7.** Flaming Gorge locale
**8.** A key might be hidden under one
**9.** Washing machine cycle
**10.** Attendant on Dionysus
**11.** Active European volcano
**12.** A purebred it's not
**13.** A veiled threat (with "or")
**18.** Certain board game turns
**19.** Friend of Homer on 'The Simpsons'
**24.** Actor Matthew ___ Gubler
**25.** 'Awesome!' in old slang
**26.** Achilles was dipped in it
**28.** City, in Saxony
**29.** Gig
**30.** A line winds in and out of it
**31.** Appeals to
**32.** Burger tycoon Ray
**33.** Virus beginning
**37.** Atrium feeder
**38.** Act like a pig
**40.** Bringing into play
**41.** Typographical flourishes
**42.** Becomes friendlier
**43.** Abbr. after Sen. Richard Lugar's name
**45.** Dramatic order to leave
**46.** 'A Fish Called Wanda' star
**49.** Early R&B group for Missy Elliott
**50.** Armor plate
**51.** ABA members
**52.** Baccarat box
**53.** Affluent Connecticut town
**54.** Chug along
**57.** A 'T' in TNT
**58.** A peeling place?
**59.** A Bobbsey

# No. 33

## Across

**1.** Actor Robert of 'Airplane!'
**5.** Actress Mason
**11.** Apron wearers, traditionally
**14.** 'Beyond the Gender Binary' author Vaid-Menon
**15.** God, in Hebrew
**16.** Alberta's ___ Island National Park
**17.** Ones on a diet
**19.** Accompaniment for some folk music
**20.** Fantasy author Canavan, author of the 'Black Magician' trilogy
**21.** Also-ran for the golden apple, in myth
**22.** A reel problem
**23.** Didn't shuffle
**25.** Actress Lords
**27.** Mottled inlay material
**32.** Common prefix with phobia
**33.** A land divided
**34.** Abbr. after an author's name, maybe
**38.** Ethan of "Boyhood"
**41.** Beginner, in lingo
**42.** African desert that includes the Skeleton Coast
**44.** Acct. figures
**46.** The three in a "threepeat"
**51.** Heroes' exploits
**52.** Avoids a big wedding
**55.** Sartre's '___ Clos'
**57.** Among
**60.** Country home
**61.** After-dinner server
**62.** Meteor shower
**64.** Ascertain
**65.** Auteur's art
**66.** Able to see right through
**67.** Beginning of a laugh
**68.** Commandeers
**69.** Aids for football kickers

## Down

**1.** Breaks for marchers
**2.** A red one is concerning
**3.** Chobani product
**4.** Big name in snowmobiles
**5.** Adapted intro?
**6.** Esau's first wife
**7.** Automatic course
**8.** Derisive acts
**9.** Zimbabwe's capital
**10.** Grafton's '___ for Alibi'
**11.** Battered and sautéed in butter
**12.** High-pH stuff
**13.** Keel extension
**18.** Gulf north of Libya
**22.** 'Bei Mir Bist Du ___'
**24.** Apply acid artistically
**26.** Act as a quizmaster
**28.** Anatomical mouths
**29.** Ann Landers was one
**30.** Actor Ayres
**31.** Area with slides
**34.** Abbr. at the end of a co. name
**35.** "A Christmas Carol" cry
**36.** Idea person
**37.** Early payphone fees
**39.** Canada hwy. distances
**40.** Lucy Ricardo's friend
**43.** Modem meas
**45.** "A Death in Vienna" author
**47.** Neighbor of Suisse
**48.** He founded the Ottoman dynasty
**49.** 'Death on the Nile' sleuth
**50.** Long, thin strip
**53.** Dissolve out
**54.** Aegean island
**55.** Command to Sweet Charlotte
**56.** Common fertilizer compound
**58.** Don Juan's mother
**59.** Greek township
**62.** Acer offerings
**63.** Aides for profs

## Across

**1.** Barracks beds
**5.** 'Baby ___ ' (2008 comedy)
**9.** Karen's love in 'Out of Africa'
**14.** Wroclaw's river, to Poles
**15.** Giant killed by Odin and his brothers
**16.** Priest's leave
**17.** A founder of the state of Israel
**18.** Aid in identifying a bird
**19.** Arcade game giant
**20.** Fraternity
**23.** Actor Gibson
**24.** Abnormal breathing
**25.** Show a different side of
**27.** A thing unto ___
**30.** Academy Award-winning Marisa
**32.** A mighty tree
**33.** Dish of thinly sliced raw meat
**37.** Souls' post-death passages
**41.** Like Norton software
**42.** Infrequent: Abbr.
**43.** Arrondissement heads?
**44.** Thread of life spinner, in myth
**47.** Artificial
**50.** Cool, '90s-style
**51.** A place to sleep
**52.** Alternative to dieting
**58.** 'Indeed!,' colloquially
**60.** Arnsberg is on it
**61.** Another name for Xiamen
**62.** Bolt from Jamaica
**63.** Mideast call to prayer
**64.** Crowdsourced map app
**65.** A sister of Marge Simpson
**66.** Cuts blades
**67.** Alternatives to saws

## Down

**1.** Afro pick, e.g
**2.** Aromatic European river?
**3.** Alvin and the Chipmunks, e.g
**4.** 'Being and Nothingness' author
**5.** I, personally
**6.** A many-splendored thing in Italy?
**7.** Chi follower
**8.** Affleck thriller
**9.** Freeloader
**10.** Abbr. after a phone no
**11.** Ronald who directed 'The Poseidon Adventure'
**12.** More maneuverable at sea
**13.** A person can take big strides with this
**21.** A.I. on Discovery One
**22.** Half of a Roald Dahl creature
**26.** Caesar conclusion
**27.** A little bit
**28.** Alpine lake
**29.** Activity in which people are not playing with a full deck
**30.** Lisbon is located at its mouth
**31.** Bobby and others
**33.** Glazed fabric
**34.** Amusing old guy
**35.** Advance at a snail's pace
**36.** Albertson's drug chain
**38.** Actress Naldi of the silents
**39.** Joseph Stalin's daughter
**40.** Actress Gaynor
**44.** Butter makers
**45.** Anita Brookner's "Hotel du ___ "
**46.** Another name for the Odawa
**47.** Bedroom shades
**48.** Bring out of slumber
**49.** Abscond with
**50.** 'Applesauce!'
**53.** Aid for a Notting Hill nanny
**54.** Anise-flavored aperitif
**55.** Big film shower
**56.** Behave like lava
**57.** Actress Carrie and others
**59.** A little thick

# No. 35

## Across

1. Albanian "dollars"
5. Back attack
10. Allergy consequence
14. Director Keshishian
15. Good for sledding, say
16. Actor Robert De ___
17. Reservists
19. Chemistry Nobelist Harold
20. A wife of Henry VIII
21. Most stylish
23. Bartending tool
25. Angel's wish
26. Appearing gnawed
29. Bit of marketing
33. 'All ___ in favor . . .'
37. A fly-by-night?
38. Absconded with
39. Loud, harsh cry
40. Affected response to an allegation
41. A Four Corners state
42. Biblical scout
44. Automated producer of spam
45. Advice to a sinner
46. Bone head?
47. Chimpersonators?
49. Benedictine monk's title
51. It rejects the caste system and idolatry
56. Dances country-western style
61. Bridgewater of jazz
62. Absolute scream
63. They keep large flocks
65. Author Sarah ___ Jewett
66. Air condition?
67. Attorney William after whom a stadium is named
68. A light one goes a long way
69. Calendar data: Abbr.
70. Ben Cartwright's second son

## Down

1. Animals on many spring greeting cards
2. 'A Cooking Egg' poet
3. Actress O'Hara with a Tony for 'The King and I'
4. Athlete in goggles
5. Barroom brawl souvenir
6. Actress Zadora
7. Aid to the poor
8. Big amount
9. Avian chatterer
10. Language of the Canadian Arctic
11. A spare one might be in the trunk
12. Abbr. in a musical score
13. Baseball Hall-of-Famer Wilhelm
18. Manning's "helmet catch" receiver
22. A puppy does it
24. Automated floor cleaner
27. Attack like an eagle
28. A-teamers
30. A traveler to Oz
31. Big family
32. Giggle sound
33. Bermuda-based business conglomerate
34. Actor Lukas of 'Witness'
35. Animals known for superior eyesight
36. Base stealer, usually
43. A rancher might pull one over a calf
45. Appealed
48. Contract addenda
50. Believer's goal
52. Pulitzer winner Seymour
53. Area explored by Lewis and Clark
54. Athlete who wrote the memoir 'Getting a Grip'
55. Arizona features
56. Ancient city undone by a large wooden horse
57. A daredevil might walk on one
58. A Chaplin
59. Able beginning?
60. A to B, say
64. A milliner makes it

# No. 36

## Across

**1.** Airer of Ken Burns documentaries
**4.** Differently ___ (challenged)
**9.** Individuals, for short
**12.** Appears dramatically
**15.** Ali of the ring
**16.** Common sport fish
**17.** Affording no illumination
**18.** Putting teeth into
**20.** Advertiser with a computer-generated mascot
**21.** Backup to a prez
**22.** A little ruff around the edges?
**23.** Bitter green vegetable
**25.** Looks good on
**27.** Put next to
**30.** Culex's cousin
**31.** Author L. Frank ___
**32.** Blogger's code
**34.** Exclamation said before sticking out the tongue
**38.** Amphion's instrument
**39.** Bad demonstrations
**41.** Easter Island statues
**42.** Allies' conference site
**44.** Command to a sled dog
**45.** Awful dancers
**46.** Analytic geometry giant
**48.** Anti-witchcraft charm
**50.** Sources of stress for many modern workers
**53.** Aerial annoyance
**54.** Atmospheric pressure unit
**55.** Acronym on a flight suit
**57.** Graph starter?
**61.** Go to the opposite side
**63.** 'Deathtrap' playwright Ira
**64.** Blocked from view
**65.** Companion of Artemis
**66.** Bring out
**67.** Celebratory cheer
**68.** Body layer
**69.** Code for Latin America's busiest airport

## Down

**1.** Advertise
**2.** Anvil, e.g
**3.** Arias, e.g.
**4.** Advil alternative
**5.** Anathema
**6.** Flotation gear
**7.** Bolted together?
**8.** D.C.'s ___ Constitution Hall
**9.** Cassandra's father
**10.** Caribbean port
**11.** Bob's cousins
**13.** Specks of space dust
**14.** Ancient Greek colonnades
**19.** Reticent
**24.** Big name in house paint
**26.** All-Star third baseman Ron
**27.** As if one knows what one is doing
**28.** Dings on a record
**29.** Finish with loops
**30.** A Lille love
**33.** It might gain you an hour
**35.** A fossil fuel
**36.** Area in some bookstores
**37.** Arts and Sciences dept
**40.** Central Asia's Tien ___ Mountains
**43.** Dumas novel "La Dame ___ Camélias"
**47.** 'Her, the fair and debonair,' to Poe
**49.** Baked beans flavor
**50.** Affected by poison ivy
**51.** Irrigation apparatus used to raise water
**52.** Adam of 'The O.C.'
**53.** Italy's largest lake
**56.** A clothes-knit union
**58.** Bank asset that's frozen?
**59.** Affable
**60.** Convenient, as some shops
**62.** Athletic field makeup

# No. 37

## Across

**1.** Attachment to "van" or "tort"
**5.** Certain worm's product
**9.** Dry up with age
**14.** Actor ____ Patrick Harris
**15.** Annoyed expression
**16.** High-pH substance
**17.** Yours and yours only
**20.** Like wearing socks with sandals, say
**21.** Excalibur's handle
**22.** Leak sources, perhaps
**23.** A pint, sometimes
**25.** 'Autrefois un ____ de Thulé' (Berlioz aria)
**26.** Miracle-____
**27.** Start of a sizable observation
**33.** Attach to the pier, say
**34.** Bering ____: Abbr
**35.** An OK city
**37.** Aer Lingus destination
**38.** George of Broadway's "La Cage aux Folles"
**41.** Entre ____
**43.** A monthly expense
**45.** Chi lead-in
**46.** A Bronte
**47.** Bridle strap utilized only on sidewalk surfaces?
**51.** Achy affliction
**53.** ?Case of the Ex? singer
**54.** Chicago's ____ Center
**55.** A bazillion jillion years
**56.** Bench press muscles, for short
**58.** Demi of pop
**63.** Typical tabloid writers
**66.** Big fan of Selena Gomez, perhaps
**67.** Bash on a beach
**68.** Action figures, e.g
**69.** Destination for a Near Eastern caravan
**70.** Avenue border, perhaps
**71.** A Guthrie

## Down

**1.** People of northeastern Canada
**2.** Ames of 'Life With Father'
**3.** Home field of the Eagles, familiarly, with "the"
**4.** A cappella group member
**5.** On the petite side
**6.** Accelerator bit
**7.** Abounding in foliage
**8.** Fermented milk drinks
**9.** Period of major fighting
**10.** Dockers' grp.
**11.** Italian custard served either hot or chilled
**12.** Aunt ____ of 'Oklahoma!'
**13.** Former Mexican president Enrique Pena ____
**18.** A horse of a different color?
**19.** Beautiful people of literature
**24.** "Bachelor" add-on
**27.** George Harrison's '____ Mine'
**28.** Alternative to rouge in roulette
**29.** Precursor
**30.** Actress Bedard
**31.** A Muse
**32.** Former kingdom of central Vietnam
**36.** Brooks & ____ (country duo)
**39.** Avis adjective
**40.** Astronomer Copernicus
**42.** Actor's workplace
**44.** Drum set
**48.** Comment put in by Putin, perhaps
**49.** Done effortlessly
**50.** Alkene derivative
**51.** Big bashes
**52.** 'Brigadoon' composer
**57.** Aretha Franklin genre
**59.** 'Apologia pro ____ Sua'
**60.** Stringed instrument of ancient Israel
**61.** 'Bye for now' in a text
**62.** Benito's bone
**64.** Adriatic or Aegean
**65.** 'Apocalypse Now' locale

# No. 38

## Across

1. Actor Jeff
6. Cpl.'s underlings
10. Cosmo and EW
14. Fellow's feminine side, says Jung
15. Acid ___
16. 'Aida' highlight
17. Rebel
20. A macadamia is one
21. Absorb the cost of
22. Boot camp busyness
23. Autocratic rule
26. Big name in country
27. Was introduced to the doctor?
32. Lame
34. Air supply
35. 'Ay, dios ___!'
36. Baroque artist Guido
37. Alternative to AOL or Juno
38. Amy Winehouse hairstyle
39. Application ending
40. A comet, to the superstitious
42. Let stand in water again
44. Violates hiring laws
47. 'Add to that . . .'
48. Aristotle of Greece
51. Absolute ruler
54. Book after Matthieu and Marc
55. 'No idea,' for short
56. Like book titles and ingredient lists
60. Adjacent to
61. Actress Negri of the silents
62. Did a whole lot of nothing
63. Citrusy-sounding Connecticut town
64. Abridge, maybe
65. 'Don't make ___!'

## Down

1. Barely audible
2. CD, e.g.?
3. They're released by the immune system
4. Aboriginal food source
5. 'Babi ___ ' (poem by Yevtushenko)
6. Audio engineer's device
7. Accurate statement
8. Abbr. following op. and loc.
9. Most derogatory
10. Extreme fan
11. Amu Darya's outflow
12. Anita Loos's autobiographical 'A ___ Like I'
13. Blurts out
18. Express again
19. Caesar's world?
24. Do chasers
25. A thing's
26. Actor Gosling
28. Anwar's successor
29. Q: Are you eligible for this job? A: Yes. ___
30. A slave of opera
31. Animal Crossing raccoon Tom
32. Actor Armisen
33. L.P.G.A. star Thompson
37. A short note
38. A smartphone has lots of them
40. Certain ship deck
41. Enter incorrectly
42. Alternative to Italian
43. A traffic jam may change it, for short
45. Author born Truman Streckfus Persons
46. Candy bar center, perhaps
49. Does nothing
50. Bus terminal postings, informally
51. Bifurcated
52. Gender identity often associated with they/them pronouns, for short
53. Bath water residue
54. Actress Taylor of 'Mystic Pizza'
57. A shower curtain hangs from one
58. Acapulco aunt
59. Big gun on a ship: Abbr

## Across

1. Act of deception
5. Church bell sounds
11. A cyclone is a big one
14. Animated feature Oscar winner after 'Zootopia'
15. Battle ___
16. A geisha may tie one on
17. Like an unfinished roof
19. A Reagan
20. Après-ski hangout
21. Aerodynamics challenge
22. Israeli conductor Daniel
23. Before analysis, after 'a'
25. Border county of New York or Pennsylvania
27. Activity for bored students and office drudges
32. Best Director nominee for 'Witness,' 'Dead Poets Society' and 'The Truman Show'
33. Actress Mallet of 'Goldfinger'
34. Abbey area
38. Begin's foreign minister
41. 'Ask ___ questions...'
42. Cosmetic injection
44. Assessment, for short
46. Earthquake measurer
51. Middle Eastern dish
52. Baseball's Nola, Judge and Hicks
55. A question of time
57. Dame ___ Te Kanawa
60. Chalon-sur-___, city SSW of Dijon
61. Ancient marauder
62. Flight simulator?
64. Airport code for O'Hare
65. Native Hawaiian
66. Actress Sommer
67. A lot of the paper
68. Andre of tennis fame
69. Act like a startled horse

## Down

1. Shape by whittling
2. Musician Oberst or playwright McPherson
3. Bad for tooth enamel
4. Genghis Khan, e.g
5. Fine wine word
6. A plan may be put on it
7. Month after Nisan
8. 'Hakuna ___'
9. Creditor's writ
10. Brutus' 'but'
11. Metz's region
12. A reed
13. 'Because of ___-Dixie' (2000 award-winning children's book)
18. Asian antelope
22. Ancient Irish alphabet
24. Applied a freezer pack to
26. ALCS mo.
28. Amanti maker
29. More ironic
30. 'A Spy in the House of Love' author
31. Arm of the U.S. Cong
34. Auto safety feature preventing skidding, for short
35. 'A Dream Within a Dream' writer
36. Allowances
37. Biological stain
39. A Gardner
40. Bay Area valley
43. Web data format
45. Asian capital that's home to Jokhang Temple
47. Art supply store stock
48. French ___ (Cayenne setting)
49. Alternative to crossing out
50. Grub around
53. WNBPA president Ogwumike
54. More desertlike
55. Amazed exclamation
56. Fiorina's replacement at HP
58. Cousins of fjords
59. Aggravates
62. Afro-Caribbean sound
63. Avril follower

## Across

**1.** Heroin, on the street
**5.** Beer features
**9.** 'Battling for Peace' author
**14.** A throne has one
**15.** Actress Taylor-Joy
**16.** Accomplished
**17.** Decem ___ (Latin decade)
**18.** Clearly outline
**19.** Vanzetti's co-defendant
**20.** Checked pattern in fabrics
**23.** AAA offering
**24.** Dress like
**25.** Boundaries
**27.** A puzzling direction
**30.** Basketball coach-turned-sportscaster Brown
**32.** Backyard pond dweller
**33.** Eponym for a mathematical pattern identified centuries earlier in India
**37.** On account (of)
**41.** Like one who can't get started fast enough
**42.** Eminem's 'Ricky Ticky ___'
**43.** Borgnine's "From Here to Eternity" role
**44.** Doctor who creates a dangerous serum
**47.** Black Lives Matter co-founder Opal
**50.** "Bed of Roses" band Bon ___
**51.** Ab ___ (from day one)
**52.** Brain specialist
**58.** A day in New Orleans
**60.** Be hesitant
**61.** Adept
**62.** Babbler?
**63.** Ado Annie, e.g
**64.** Amount a washing machine holds
**65.** Adjusts soundtracks
**66.** Double-timed
**67.** Basic beliefs

## Down

**1.** Any member of the Safavid dynasty
**2.** Appropriate rhyme for 'Reno'
**3.** Aboriginal Japanese
**4.** An American in Mexico
**5.** Chancho en piedra and pico de gallo, e.g
**6.** Army groups
**7.** Big name in label makers
**8.** Juan's health
**9.** Soft shawl
**10.** Author LeShan
**11.** Prefix meaning "straight"
**12.** Attraction in Bay Lake, Fla
**13.** Has capacity for
**21.** A couple in Mexico?
**22.** Accompaniment for a fife
**26.** A drummer keeps it
**27.** Sony co-founder Morita
**28.** Quadrennial polit. event
**29.** Anne who writes of vampires
**30.** Baseball's Nomo
**31.** Above, in Aachen
**33.** Fiber-rich fruits
**34.** Accra or Agra
**35.** Air-condition
**36.** With: Abbr
**38.** Golden fish stocked in ornamental pools
**39.** Ones who are never out of order?
**40.** Composer Erik
**44.** Gave a shock
**45.** Annual video game competition, for short
**46.** African capital southwest of Kampala
**47.** Archaeological discoveries
**48.** Biological egg source
**49.** Alfred E. Neuman, for one
**50.** Angelina of 'Kung Fu Panda'
**53.** 'That is ... not looking good'
**54.** Anise-flavored apéritif popular in Turkey and the Balkans
**55.** Native Nigerians
**56.** A four-RBI hit
**57.** Baseball's Radcliffe and Williams
**59.** Bashful associate?

# No. 41

## Across

**1.** Air Force heroes
**5.** Bits in a byte, e.g
**10.** Annual '500'
**14.** Easily fooled person
**15.** Bridge officer on the original Enterprise
**16.** Edible algae used to wrap sushi
**17.** Blurred
**19.** Ado
**20.** Vinegar radical
**21.** Beats badly
**23.** Designed to increase traction
**25.** Island off India's coast
**26.** Actor Joe of 'My Cousin Vinny'
**29.** Accelerator or brake
**33.** Angel's dream
**37.** Black side of a circle, in Chinese philosophy
**38.** Attack anonymously
**39.** Beguiling trick
**40.** Army missions
**41.** Chainer of Prometheus
**42.** Ancient region north of Sumer
**44.** Act the snoop
**45.** Goethe character who makes a pact with the devil
**46.** Country singer Crystal
**47.** A school might be found using it
**49.** Attachment to "pend"
**51.** Red choices
**56.** Pawn place
**61.** Abruzzi's locale
**62.** Alternative to Chinese or Indian
**63.** Ephemeral
**65.** Arctic ____ (migratory bird)
**66.** Air a "Seinfeld" episode
**67.** A mini shows it
**68.** All in favor
**69.** Bits
**70.** Leaky noise

## Down

**1.** Afghan or Thai
**2.** A third of quince
**3.** Ems River port
**4.** Barbecue accessories
**5.** Extend beyond
**6.** A.L. and N.L. city
**7.** Large containers for wine
**8.** A good shoe supports it
**9.** Anachronous
**10.** Something caught in the air
**11.** Acronymic nickname for Bourbon Street's city
**12.** Adam Sandler's "Hotel Transylvania" role
**13.** Athlete's sudden loss of ability, informally
**18.** Air spirit, in folklore
**22.** Balm targets
**24.** 'Hearts and minds' activities, in military slang
**27.** Widely used antibiotic brand
**28.** Attuned
**30.** Diable battler
**31.** Bird of Paradise constellation
**32.** Avoiding the risk that
**33.** Appropriate initials of 'stuff we all get'
**34.** Brzezinski of 'Morning Joe'
**35.** Boozer
**36.** Arctic cover-ups
**43.** Ditat --- (God enriches)
**45.** Brief chapters?
**48.** Abductors in a tabloid story
**50.** Brittle fragment (var.)
**52.** Amasses, with "up"
**53.** Book and film title character surnamed Gatzoyiannis
**54.** Antler branches
**55.** An anagram for "asset"
**56.** Address starter
**57.** Footballer Michael featured in 'The Blind Side'
**58.** Beloved, in 'Rigoletto'
**59.** Above
**60.** Equal: Prefix
**64.** A pencil that's mostly eraser

# No. 42

## Across

**1.** Pollutant concentration meas

**4.** Catch on

**9.** Animal going to market, maybe

**12.** Animosities that may span generations

**15.** Believer in an Ethiopian Zion

**16.** Canadian prov.

**17.** Beginning for "violet" or "sound"

**18.** Press persistently

**20.** Accra-to-Khartoum dir

**21.** Big water pipe

**22.** ATTEMPT A BREAK-IN

**23.** A native of

**25.** Cash-back come-ons

**27.** English author Bulwer-____

**30.** Will Smith's singing/acting son

**31.** 'A Love Like ____' (Barbra Streisand album)

**32.** An awkward, stupid person

**34.** Sets of undealt cards in a certain game

**38.** Abandon, as a subject

**39.** Belgian battle site of World War I

**41.** Address for a king

**42.** Arctic duck

**44.** A former Spice Girl

**45.** Achieved greater proportions

**46.** Bit of dirt

**48.** Bearded perennials

**50.** Author of 'The Praise of Folly'

**53.** City in the Ukraine

**54.** Lead-in to -drome

**55.** Bhagavad ____ (Hindu scripture)

**57.** Offends

**61.** Lengthens

**63.** Bomber ____ Gay

**64.** Air chief marshal's org

**65.** Silver-leaved tree

**66.** Bad-looking person?

**67.** Palindromic alternative to .exe

**68.** Affirmative responses

**69.** Abbr. in two state names

## Down

**1.** 'Bah, humbug!'

**2.** Big name in educational funding

**3.** Conductor Riccardo

**4.** Andersen contemporary

**5.** Alien spacecraft in an Arthur C. Clarke tale

**6.** Pronounces breathily

**7.** High on pot

**8.** A double bogey is two over it

**9.** Baseball catcher's position

**10.** A jigger is bigger than this

**11.** Best-seller list heading

**13.** Bartender?

**14.** Iliac attachment

**19.** The second Monday in October, in Canada

**24.** Adverb in sale flyers

**26.** Wanna-____

**27.** Abundant store

**28.** Chess master Averbakh

**29.** Beat a path

**30.** Case studier

**33.** Hot and cold, for example

**35.** A show of vanity

**36.** A persimmon grows on one

**37.** Adds a border to a quilt, e.g

**40.** Back-alley blade

**43.** A spirit

**47.** Longtime Zimbabwean leader

**49.** Amorous guy

**50.** Chris in the International Tennis Hall of Fame

**51.** Advice to a type-A person

**52.** Among the clouds

**53.** Cuts with light

**56.** BBC receiver

**58.** Bow out of a poker hand

**59.** Abominable hopper

**60.** Cutty ____

**62.** Applicant for a civil union, maybe

# No. 43

## Across

**1.** A number one
**5.** Acts human
**9.** Antilles island
**14.** Fashion house known for its paisley patterns
**15.** A less-than-average tide
**16.** Actress Saoirse of "Brooklyn"
**17.** Grimm brothers fairy tale
**20.** Annual San Antonio celebration
**21.** Carefully pack (away)
**22.** A first name among first ladies
**23.** A sleeve covers it
**25.** A compliment might give it a boost
**26.** Antigone is spelled with two
**27.** Like some cross-dressers
**33.** A resting place
**34.** "Achtung Baby" co-producer
**35.** Big-hearted
**37.** Band whose name sounds like a vegetable
**38.** Hardy hog breed
**41.** Eric the Red's son
**43.** All-Star Martinez
**45.** Raphael's weapon in "Teenage Mutant Ninja Turtles"
**46.** Cape fox
**47.** Informal social gathering
**51.** Certain ladies' room
**53.** 'America's Most Wanted' airer
**54.** Fraternal patriotic org
**55.** Arcadian god
**56.** Chop ___
**58.** April, May and June, to Daisy Duck
**63.** Playground activity
**66.** Alligator's prey
**67.** Bavarian river
**68.** Annoying little squirt
**69.** Ages badly
**70.** Acronym for fighting organized crime
**71.** Actress Harper of 'No Country for Old Men'

## Down

**1.** A slave, not a wave
**2.** Cartoon 'Yuck!'
**3.** 'Coffee, Tea ___' (1960's best seller)
**4.** As a maximum
**5.** Blew up
**6.** Abbr. next to a telephone number
**7.** Alley crawlers
**8.** Dealt with maliciously
**9.** Foyer enhancement
**10.** Author Asquith of children's books
**11.** Bad behavior
**12.** Major Chinese internet company
**13.** Christie and Karenina
**18.** Airline info, for short
**19.** Area between an upper and lower deck
**24.** A choice location
**27.** Admonisher's sound
**28.** A cube has one
**29.** Golfers Ernie Els and Retief Goosen, for two
**30.** Norse goddess married to Balder
**31.** Ancient raiders
**32.** Gulf of Aqaba city
**36.** A laser might read it
**39.** Acorn droppers
**40.** Burrito flavoring
**42.** Disgusted exclamation
**44.** Compensates for
**48.** Afternoon hour for tea
**49.** Academy town
**50.** 'Acoustic Soul' singer India. ___
**51.** One making a choice
**52.** Third largest city in South Korea
**57.** Ashram teacher
**59.** Archaic "formerly"
**60.** Art film theater
**61.** A chimpanzee astronaut
**62.** Army three-stripers: Abbr
**64.** Annual celebration during which sweeping is taboo
**65.** Case studier, slangily

# No. 44

## Across

1. Austrian composer Berg
6. Feigned
10. Abel's killer
14. Auto repair chain
15. Acoustical bounce
16. Everybody, to Erich
17. One dealing with issues
20. Actor Gorcey
21. Moroccan city known as the Athens of Africa
22. Prestigious magazine awards
23. Argentine writer ___ Sábato
26. British general in America, Thomas
27. Arnold Schwarzenegger, Robert Patrick and Kristanna Loken?
32. Bedsheet fabric
34. A language spoken in Scotland
35. British miler Sebastian
36. Galatea's love
37. African plant whose leaves are chewed as a stimulant
38. New Jersey university
39. Anemic
40. Beat in an upset
42. In the direction of
44. Bad occupation for Sleepy?
47. 'Pics ___ didn't happen' (slangy challenge)
48. Acts frugally around the holidays, say
51. Beat at the track
54. Dram
55. Big camping gear retailer
56. Security requests
60. Appease fully
61. Celebrity chef Matsuhisa
62. All, in old-time stage directions
63. Beheld
64. Astonished exclamations
65. Toddler's training site

## Down

1. Abundant
2. Bar code reader
3. Taking a stab at?
4. Adapter designation
5. Classic Japanese drama form
6. Astronomical streaker
7. Adolph ___, creator of the slogan 'All the News That's Fit to Print'
8. Amigo of Fidel
9. Hanbok Day celebrants
10. It's easy to swallow
11. Et ___ ("and others")
12. Actress Steppat of 'On Her Majesty's Secret Service'
13. Acrobats' safety gear
18. Again and again
19. Aquarium bother
24. Alimony check cashers
25. Abbr. in an office address
26. Belted
28. Connoted
29. Beach
30. Air show sound
31. Bad button to hit by accident
32. Already cut, as lumber
33. Antioxidant berry
37. Four, in prescriptions
38. Famous movie river
40. Classic Fender guitar, for short
41. Interlacing
42. Angle denoter, in math
43. Amazed initials
45. Kind of viper or owl
46. Long-tubed flower
49. A golden rule, e.g
50. Actress Spacek
51. Auvers-sur-___, last home of Vincent van Gogh
52. Son of Saddam
53. Beret filler
54. Be in harmony (with)
57. A McCoy, to a Hatfield
58. Big ___ (circus)
59. Abbr. preceding a person's POV

# No. 45

## Across

1. Acapulco appetizer
5. Apparatus for two
11. A person who's short might run to it
14. Acted and spoke like
15. Cave temple site of India
16. Aid in getting back on track
17. Butterfly-to-be
19. A hatchet is a small one
20. Central Florida city
21. Amphilochus, for one
22. Cell at sea
23. A lines, e.g
25. Cattlemen of Kenya
27. In a servile manner
32. Christmas holly
33. AT&T, for one
34. Character in "The Good Earth"
38. Apt rhyme of 'fleck'
41. Connecticut senator Christopher
42. Early name for up-tempo jazz
44. Actor Ifans of 'The Amazing Spider-Man'
46. College commencement speaker
51. Actress Woodard
52. Lace ends
55. Aces may finish them off
57. Give ___ on the shoulder
60. Baryshnikov nickname
61. Another cal. column heading
62. Dinosaur whose name means 'winged finger'
64. Catullus's 'Odi et ___'
65. Surface again
66. Town outside of Buffalo
67. Popular anxiety drug, informally
68. An antonym for "restores"
69. Appreciates

## Down

1. Al pastor servings
2. At a fast clip, poetically
3. Aid in breaching castle walls
4. Antarctic penguin
5. Acct. akin to an IRA
6. Ancient Greek land that hosted the Olympics
7. Activist Hearns
8. Formal and dignified
9. Ancient debarkation site
10. 'A defeat for humanity,' per Pope John Paul II
11. Cadillac Ranch city
12. Airplanes do it
13. Common digital video format
18. 'Baby Beluga' singer
22. Acted sheepish?
24. Le Cordon Bleu seasonings
26. Avoid elimination in musical chairs
28. A squat, e.g.
29. Apply
30. Certain readout, for short
31. Letter after teth
34. One of the Wright brothers, for short
35. A grassy glade
36. Surgical removal procedure
37. Airs during the holidays
39. Actor John of 'American Pie' films
40. Actress Sedgwick
43. Adobe document suffix
45. Arithmetic series symbol
47. More angry
48. It's usually abbreviated 'c.'
49. Arlo's restaurant
50. Be cozy
53. Bouillabaisse seasoning
54. Casa contents
55. Tunisian port
56. 'Anything Goes' dame
58. Actress Meyers and others
59. A model strikes one
62. Adolescent lead-in
63. Académie ___ Beaux-Arts

# No. 46

## Across

**1.** Level ground, in a way
**5.** Atlantic swimmers
**9.** Third-largest of the Philippines
**14.** 'A Death in the Family' author
**15.** Actress Lane
**16.** Mainlander, in Hawaii
**17.** Banca d'Italia unit, once
**18.** Alligator ___
**19.** Act introducer
**20.** Rural vista
**23.** Cabinet dept. launched under LBJ
**24.** Action film weapons
**25.** Presumptuous
**27.** Condition of affairs
**30.** Big name in china
**32.** 'A Hymn to ___' ('My Fair Lady' song)
**33.** Fiancée, say
**37.** Like questions of what is knowable
**41.** Like dollhouse furnishings
**42.** Abbr. before a credit card date
**43.** Amazingly fun time
**44.** A good dessert to split?
**47.** Filmdom's Nastassja
**50.** Gertz of 'The Lost Boys'
**51.** Aga Khan's son
**52.** Community of Web journals
**58.** Accessory for a bride, maybe
**60.** Cardinal number (fifth power of ten)
**61.** Alpine climber
**62.** Ancient Greek tongue: Var.
**63.** Arraignment entry
**64.** Castor and Pollux's mother
**65.** After-school nosh
**66.** A breeze
**67.** City adjacent to Provo

## Down

**1.** Absorbent application
**2.** Charge for currency exchange
**3.** Tanzanian mountain
**4.** Bit of cushioning
**5.** Alternative to culottes
**6.** Acts the flunky
**7.** Bus. degrees
**8.** Bandar ___ Begawan (Brunei's capital)
**9.** Border collie, for one
**10.** Texas school
**11.** Chewy rice confection
**12.** Aboriginal Alaskan
**13.** Frail
**21.** China's Lao-___
**22.** Cathedral of Florence
**26.** Actress Gilpin of "Frasier"
**27.** A son of Noah
**28.** Ceremonial tent
**29.** Bygone dictator
**30.** A belt at the bar
**31.** Achromous
**33.** ABC Radio host
**34.** Absolutely nailed
**35.** Biologists' groupings
**36.** L'Eiger, e.g
**38.** A boy and his sis
**39.** Reply with sass
**40.** 'Add to cart' business
**44.** Amble with an attitude
**45.** A count manager
**46.** Creatio ex ___ (Christian tenet)
**47.** Beckinsale and Mulgrew
**48.** Troy, to Homer
**49.** White-striped antelope
**50.** Good ones are cracked
**53.** Ancient wine jug
**54.** Annual Met event
**55.** Celebrity hairstylist Jose
**56.** Counsel, in English dialect
**57.** Academic challenge
**59.** Ansel Adams documentarian Burns

# No. 47

## Across

1. Actress ___ Pinkett Smith
5. Greek goddess of chance
10. Ancient alpaca herder
14. All tucked in
15. Angers, with 'up'
16. American-born Jordanian queen
17. Takes the edge off?
19. At the ocean's bottom, as a ship
20. Bone-related
21. Conference room events
23. Acupuncturist's supply
25. Check alternative?
26. Rumbly tummy soother
29. Big brand of kitchen knives
33. Beverage in blue cans
37. Calder Cup org
38. John Paul II's first name
39. Concerning the congregation
40. Bad boy in "Toy Story"
41. Like a Salmon P. Chase bill, slangily
42. Acidic
44. Common calculator button
45. Alternative to Travelers
46. A crowd, it's said
47. 'An ally has been ___' (bad news in League of Legends)
49. Certain trader, for short
51. Cutting-edge medical device
56. Aileron attachments
61. Bass role in a Gilbert & Sullivan opera
62. Dream of Debussy
63. Bullied
65. Abbr. after N. or S.
66. Four-time NBA All-Star Leonard
67. Achiever of many goals
68. Avoid work, in Britain
69. Abbr. in some group names
70. For no good reason

## Down

1. Argo pilot
2. Badmouth
3. Al ___
4. Calculated a sum
5. Historic destination in County Kerry, Ireland
6. Bark like a chihuahua
7. Blondie drummer Burke
8. Accounted for, in a way
9. Anglo-Saxon kingdom
10. Imply
11. A follower?
12. Capitol Hill gp
13. Biblical vessels
18. Sense organs in insects
22. Camping menace
24. Bursts of energy
27. Peter ___, co-founder of PayPal
28. Appellation for winter
30. Allowance for waste
31. Didi of "Grease"
32. Acrobatic Korbut
33. Area map
34. A head
35. Anchorage area
36. Many roller coaster riders
43. A Bobbsey twin
45. Alvy's love interest in a Woody Allen film
48. Like "To be or not to be"
50. Cake similar to a kokosh
52. African animal with striped hindquarters
53. Held in suspense
54. Beckham Jr. of the Browns
55. Cruiserweight boxing champion James ___
56. Abbr. on folk song sheet music
57. Action film hero Williams
58. 'A Little Bitty Tear' singer
59. Adjustable garments
60. Bearers of piglets
64. A question of identity

## Across

**1.** A lot of mil. personnel
**5.** Misjudges a push door
**10.** Choice assignment
**14.** Actress Michelle of 'Crazy Rich Asians'
**15.** Allegheny River city
**16.** Nuke-detecting U.S. satellite
**17.** Amusement park lure
**18.** Steam locomotive feature
**20.** A Guinness world record adjective
**22.** Apply for
**23.** Air show formation
**24.** Academy Award nomination, informally
**25.** City planners
**27.** Cloudophobia?
**33.** Big Spanish-language newspaper
**34.** Actor's minimum
**35.** Marcus or Winfred of the N.F.L.
**39.** Any symphony
**41.** Actress Gadot
**42.** Aft's antithesis
**43.** Knowledgeable on arcane details of a subject
**45.** A brother of Prometheus
**48.** A lot of popular music nowadays
**49.** Order to Onassis to block a brand of underwear?
**52.** Less apt to trust
**55.** Cadence call
**56.** 'Beg pardon?'
**57.** Head: Ger
**60.** Onetime pickling liquid
**64.** Ones who aren't easy on the I's
**67.** Major-___
**68.** Adriatic resort
**69.** Big name in Chinese history
**70.** Agate variety
**71.** Soupy color
**72.** Airline once said to be 'ready when you are'
**73.** 'Holy ___!'

## Down

**1.** Arsonist, in brief
**2.** Bit of bridal attire
**3.** A husband of Elizabeth Taylor
**4.** Comic book queen of the jungle
**5.** Aspiring prof, maybe
**6.** Cathedral city of southwest Germany
**7.** A majority of August births
**8.** Africa's ___ Chad
**9.** Blessed act?
**10.** Beetle Bailey's rank: Abbr
**11.** Army vacation
**12.** Abdominal pain producer
**13.** Arrives in time for
**19.** Article of female tennis attire
**21.** Alkies
**26.** Dix minus un
**27.** 'A Black Lady Sketch ___'
**28.** Hiker's map, briefly
**29.** Miler turned congressman
**30.** Adventure stories
**31.** Chief on "Get Smart"
**32.** Adele hit that won Grammys for Song and Record of the Year

**36.** Brought into being
**37.** Aberdeen hillside
**38.** Turn-of-the-season mos
**40.** 'Jessie' actress Jackson
**44.** Northern California town once home to the palindromic ___ Bakery
**46.** Loss of speaking ability
**47.** Holy Ark's location
**50.** Attended to pressing matters?
**51.** Simian world
**52.** Any element in the first column of the periodic table, except hydrogen
**53.** March in a Saul Bellow book
**54.** Carlton was her doorman
**58.** Bench material
**59.** Autumn
**61.** 'This will ___ further'
**62.** Pentane derivative
**63.** Art-rock's ___ Music
**65.** Pet cat, in British lingo
**66.** Abyssinian or Persian

# No. 49

## Across

**1.** Aoki of golf
**5.** 'Ain't Got No' musical
**9.** Anchor line's hole
**14.** Animated character helped by Gill, Bloat, Peach and Bubbles
**15.** Arena for the Kings
**16.** Astronaut Ellen
**17.** Baby-boomer series that starred Ken Olin
**20.** Addresses a convention, for example
**21.** A crane might hover over one
**22.** Baby boomers, with 'the'
**23.** 'All aboard!' area: Abbr.
**25.** 'A Black Lady Sketch Show' producer Issa
**26.** Acronym for linked computers
**27.** Impromptu
**33.** Be afflicted with
**34.** Abbr. after Kennedy or Lincoln
**35.** Brand advertised as 'the forbidden fragrance'
**37.** Day before a Jewish holiday
**38.** IRA's kin
**41.** Alternative to penne
**43.** Bittersweet coating
**45.** Bao ___ (former Vietnamese emperor)
**46.** A lid usually covers it at night
**47.** Cinnamon sugar cookie
**51.** Water, chemically
**53.** G.R.F.'s choice for VP
**54.** Average of tre and nove
**55.** Antismoking gp
**56.** Abbr. of urgency
**58.** Biblically named Michigan college
**63.** Failure to adhere to moral principles
**66.** Actress Emma Roberts, to Julia Roberts
**67.** Affaires d'___
**68.** A cluttered one is a sign of a cluttered mind, it's said
**69.** Assigned duties
**70.** Basketball officials
**71.** Animals in hibernación

## Down

**1.** A big fan of
**2.** Ilse's 'very'
**3.** 'What ___ mind reader?'
**4.** Astronomy's ___ cloud
**5.** Needle setting, perhaps
**6.** Aristotle's '___ Rhetorica'
**7.** A mouse may be drawn to it
**8.** Cesar ___, classic player of the Joker
**9.** Guinness Book weather record category
**10.** 'Alas' in Augsburg
**11.** Eggbeater
**12.** Actress Braga
**13.** Boston-based columnist Margery
**18.** A crucible is a hard one
**19.** A bibilical son of Rebekah
**24.** A chip before the deal
**27.** A miss
**28.** Arm of the Amazon
**29.** Gives too much information
**30.** Composer Ethelbert
**31.** Become weatherworn
**32.** Region of Italy that includes Rome
**36.** Abbr. that rhymes with 'bill,' appropriately
**39.** Elongated, heavily armored fish
**40.** Low-lying areas?
**42.** Advert's ending?
**44.** Measures of newspaper ad space
**48.** A.T.M. supply
**49.** Bowl for mixing wine and water in ancient Greece
**50.** Adds lubrication to
**51.** Be there in spirit?
**52.** All, to Augustus
**57.** A Rose
**59.** Beginning for China
**60.** Certain necklines
**61.** A gas from the past
**62.** 'Bad!' sounds
**64.** 'Blech!'
**65.** Awkward one

# No. 50

## Across

1. Bros
6. Barrio greeting
10. Campus fig.
14. Actress Davalos
15. First king of Phliasia, in myth
16. Best-selling erotic novelist ___ Leigh
17. Without reservations
20. 'A guy walks into a ___ ...'
21. Acapulco gold
22. Having no charge
23. Boiled
26. A surfboard rides it
27. Jockey's other job?
32. Blot on one's reputation
34. 'Close My Eyes Forever' singer ___ Ford
35. Abbr. in a military address
36. Big name in computer-based audio hardware
37. Awacs component: Abbr
38. Actor Ed of 'Daniel Boone'
39. Chess champ before and after Botvinnik
40. Abreast of
42. Assets
44. Crazy researcher?
47. Coat for corn
48. Of a speaker's platform
51. Arrange by categories
54. Cologne conjunction
55. Abbr. on a film box
56. The glow of a glowworm
60. Blue, in Bogotá
61. Absorb's opposite
62. Ancient Greek metropolis
63. Antibody sources
64. Allure publisher Conde ___
65. Bonaventures, e.g

## Down

1. Applies crudely
2. Arm supports
3. Without youthful vigor
4. Intro to biology?
5. Angelo or Antonio
6. Afro, bun or bob
7. 'For here ___ go?'
8. China's Chou En-___
9. Like a silent letter
10. American fleet
11. Deeply massage
12. Border of a coat of arms
13. Actress Alice of old Hollywood
18. 'A merry heart ___ good like a medicine': Proverbs
19. Girlfriend, in Granada
24. By way of, briefly
25. Ad ___
26. Devices sold with motion sensors
28. 'Captain Blood' star
29. They may be pulled by runners
30. A masked competitor waves it
31. Antarctic explorer James
32. Outgoing email initials
33. Bygone big birds
37. Charge far too much
38. Czech Rep. neighbor
40. African political movement
41. Box fillers
42. Goes none too quickly
43. City in Arthur C. Clarke's 'The City and the Stars'
45. Spiny cactus
46. Actor Will of 'Up All Night'
49. Accouterment for Fred of 'Scooby-Doo'
50. Clay deposit
51. Arab garments
52. Assess (with "up")
53. Bad way to turn
54. As one, at Orly
57. ABBA's '___ Marionette'
58. Auto shaft attachment
59. A cause for Steinem

# No. 51

## Across

**1.** Attach (onto)
**5.** Cocktail word that means "strained"
**11.** Accusing of misconduct
**14.** First capital of Japan
**15.** Audrey Tautou title role
**16.** A Minor Prophet: Abbr.
**17.** Creator of short sentences?
**19.** Cook chicken, in a way
**20.** Cheery
**21.** Amy Winehouse's 'Stronger ___ Me'
**22.** Alternative facts
**23.** Adding kick to
**25.** Twain's ___ Joe
**27.** So sad
**32.** Actress ___ Ali Khan
**33.** California's San ___ County
**34.** Alike
**38.** Bagless vacuum brand
**41.** Destructive Hindu god (var.)
**42.** 'American Pie' beauty
**44.** 'A Sorta Fairytale' singer Tori
**46.** Like some cruises
**51.** Doesn't draw
**52.** Broadcasters
**55.** Dance-a-___
**57.** Act the fool
**60.** Nettie's sister in 'The Color Purple'
**61.** Barnyard bleat
**62.** It might be in a jam
**64.** 'A Raisin in the ___' (Hansberry play)
**65.** Actress Andress
**66.** Baker, at times
**67.** Abbr. of politeness
**68.** Appropriate, as behavior
**69.** A shopping mall has lots of these

## Down

**1.** Bump on a log
**2.** Lips, in Latin
**3.** Briscoe's portrayer on 'Law & Order'
**4.** Last Hitchcock film with Tippi Hedren
**5.** Basketball's King James, for one
**6.** Act the abridger
**7.** Actress Remini
**8.** Aquila's brightest star
**9.** Last name of famed quintuplets
**10.** Atmosphere: Prefix
**11.** G37 automaker
**12.** Adult filly
**13.** M.D.
**18.** Bunsen burner relatives
**22.** Haas of 'Inception'
**24.** Alum
**26.** Ad-lib, musically
**28.** An encouraging word
**29.** Forming a bottom layer
**30.** Battle Born State: Abbr.
**31.** Antelope of the Himalayas
**34.** 'A Bug's Life' bug
**35.** Bright, to Brecht
**36.** Moscow natives
**37.** Chiffon or voile used to make curtains
**39.** German grandmother
**40.** 'Ali' actress Gaye
**43.** A fist might represent A or S in it: Abbr.
**45.** Cinnamon unit
**47.** Appeal to earnestly
**48.** African bloodsucker
**49.** Conciliatory
**50.** Popular sports coupe
**53.** More abounding
**54.** Advisers of old
**55.** Abbr. in a recipe
**56.** Act the trucker
**58.** Unfermented grape juice
**59.** Act the fink
**62.** Aberrant Steinbeck vehicle
**63.** Actor Liotta

# No. 52

**Across**

**1.** Arctic explorer Louise Arner ___

**5.** 'Behold!' to Brutus

**9.** Anticipatory times

**14.** Brynhildr's brother, in myth

**15.** Aligned, after 'in'

**16.** Wheel-bound victim of Zeus

**17.** 'Big Brother' host Julie

**18.** Actress Powers

**19.** Bygone Olds

**20.** When some kings and queens are crowned

**23.** 'A leopard can't change its spots,' e.g.

**24.** Also-___

**25.** Burnout consequence

**27.** Dramatist Paul who won a Tony for 'Morning's at Seven'

**30.** Electron-transferring process

**32.** A few lines on one's Twitter profile, say

**33.** Misses overseas

**37.** Band member

**41.** Plato and others

**42.** Actor Daniel ___-Lewis

**43.** Ever so slightly

**44.** Goddess of widsom

**47.** Airport landing area

**50.** Boss on a shield

**51.** Admiring fear

**52.** What animal bites may cause

**58.** Montreal suburb

**60.** Attention-getter, in some rooms

**61.** Floozy

**62.** Drummer Gene

**63.** 'Adam ___'

**64.** Long, narrow shoe size

**65.** 'Big yikes'

**66.** Abbr. in a closely held business

**67.** Acted like a rat

**Down**

**1.** 'Ascension Oratorio' composer

**2.** Early Roman emperor

**3.** Matter in the Big Bang theory

**4.** Barcelona bucks

**5.** Irish equivalent of Edward

**6.** Bones up

**7.** E. ___

**8.** Actor McGregor of 'Trainspotting'

**9.** Group migration

**10.** Guns N' Roses frontman ___ Rose

**11.** Brolin's 'Life in Pieces' co-star

**12.** Author Lofts

**13.** Covered in frozen flakes

**21.** Airport rental

**22.** Actress Gal

**26.** Angle between a leafstalk and a stem

**27.** Accessories whose colors may indicate rank

**28.** Chinese, in prefixes

**29.** Anjou alternative

**30.** Athlete/model Gabrielle

**31.** Austrian river to the Danube

**33.** Goo-goo-eyed, old-style

**34.** All competition

**35.** Bald-eagle link

**36.** Affliction also known as a hordeolum

**38.** Airport conveyance

**39.** West Bank city

**40.** A city in central New York

**44.** Blows away

**45.** Instagram hashtag accompanying a nostalgic photo

**46.** Construction lifts

**47.** Like Eric Rohmer movies

**48.** Alerted to

**49.** Burlesque show

**50.** Hives

**53.** All-Century Team member

**54.** Admirer at a distance

**55.** Latin oils

**56.** "Cats" director Trevor

**57.** All-male

**59.** Coll.-level classes

# No. 53

## Across

**1.** Border river between China and Russia
**5.** Appliance with burners
**10.** In ___ (stuck)
**14.** Alternative to a brewski
**15.** Slow as molasses
**16.** A.P.R.-lowering option
**17.** Put in the spotlight
**19.** Abbr. on an old map of the West
**20.** Slangy smoke
**21.** Certain designer dog
**23.** Alphabetical, e.g
**25.** As in text (Lat.)
**26.** Common praenomen among Roman emperors
**29.** Abu ___
**33.** Astronaut's workplace
**37.** African game
**38.** Dava ___, author of the best seller 'Longitude'
**39.** Baba ___ (Gilda Radner character)
**40.** A drop in the ocean?
**41.** Backbone of a boat
**42.** Back street
**44.** Aloe vera liquid
**45.** Indoor balls
**46.** 'Blame It on the ___ Nova'
**47.** Architectural crossbeam
**49.** 'Adorable!'
**51.** Search, as at a sale
**56.** Liquor with a double-headed eagle logo
**61.** Gasoline choice
**62.** Accommodating to night owls
**63.** Highway no-no
**65.** Animal in the sky
**66.** Airy areas of hotels
**67.** It's above a parakeet's beak
**68.** English author Elinor
**69.** Belgian city or province
**70.** Apricot and tangerine

## Down

**1.** Boat with a message
**2.** Athlete who's not dashing?
**3.** Anarchic
**4.** Baton ___, Louisiana
**5.** Bridal wreath shrub
**6.** Adult walrus's weight, approximately
**7.** Agreement word
**8.** A presidential power
**9.** Close watchers
**10.** Food with a heart
**11.** Army transport
**12.** A 'do seen at Woodstock
**13.** Abstract artist Joan
**18.** Aunt ___, despised relative of Harry Potter
**22.** Audience for Cocomelon, the most-viewed YouTube channel in the U.S
**24.** Abridged collection
**27.** Open a cage
**28.** Sort of performance
**30.** But, in Berlin
**31.** Bit of food ... or feud?
**32.** Contents of Pandora's box, except for hope
**33.** Absorbent stick
**34.** Alto lead-in?
**35.** Belt hole makers
**36.** Certain section
**43.** Act that's 'contagious'
**45.** Ancient Greek city with a mythical lion
**48.** Crass
**50.** 'Das Rheingold' god
**52.** Alternative to a lighter
**53.** A fond farewell
**54.** Action or drama, e.g
**55.** A cylinder has two
**56.** Animal similar to a snail
**57.** Calcium-rich soil
**58.** Adjective for a yellow polka dot bikini
**59.** Last wife of Bluebeard
**60.** Al dente
**64.** Actress and 'Unhomed Belongings' artist Lucy

## Across

**1.** Tapestry threads
**6.** California's ___ Valley
**10.** Applet language
**14.** Old serf
**15.** Atone for a semester of goofing off
**16.** Alternative to DOS or Windows
**17.** A-list
**18.** A chest often has a large one
**19.** Bowlful at a Japanese restaurant
**20.** Apt example of this puzzle's theme
**22.** A is the best one
**23.** Financial advisor Orman
**24.** Be completely preoccupied
**26.** "Amen" deacon
**30.** A.&P. and Amex, e.g.
**31.** Acid container
**32.** Abrupt transition
**33.** Author Shere
**35.** Accelerates, with 'up'
**39.** Held in high regard
**41.** Flowering shrub with white or pink flowers
**43.** Apple genius?
**44.** Ex-Cleveland QB Brian
**46.** Become a traitor
**47.** Aussie boot brand
**49.** A lot of bucks ... or the Bucks, briefly
**50.** Rama's wife, in Hinduism
**51.** One catching the game
**54.** Adrienne Rich or Nikki Giovanni
**56.** Abdominal and lower-back muscles, collectively
**57.** Proselytizer
**63.** Hillary Clinton aide Abedin
**64.** Actress Rowlands
**65.** Aggressively virile
**66.** Architect Sir Christopher ___
**67.** A Brady kid
**68.** Cheap so-and-so
**69.** Acts the Good Samaritan
**70.** Base of an arch
**71.** Arrange hair

## Down

**1.** Excite, as an appetite
**2.** Challenging to corner
**3.** Basic gymnastics move
**4.** Add (up)
**5.** Agonizes (over)
**6.** Some sufferers of personality disorders
**7.** Most furious
**8.** Rapping minister
**9.** Ad-libbed comedy
**10.** Energizing impetuses
**11.** Doddering
**12.** Documents shown at border checkpoints
**13.** Cellular transmitters
**21.** Frilly trim
**25.** A one-hit Wonder he's not
**26.** Bad condition for a tire
**27.** Another attempt
**28.** Beta carotene sources
**29.** Devotees of fine dining
**34.** Bond's field
**36.** Demigod in "Moana"
**37.** Apt to mouth off
**38.** Arabian peninsula capital
**40.** 'Afro Puffs' rapper The Lady of ___
**42.** Co-owner of the Pequod
**45.** Assemble, as a jury
**48.** Style of shorthand, informally
**51.** Agenda's beginning or end
**52.** 'Bay City Blues' star Michael
**53.** Available to shoot
**55.** Fill-in workers or this puzzle's theme
**58.** Florida's ___ Beach
**59.** Addition to café
**60.** Covered in slime, e.g
**61.** Author Silverstein
**62.** Barreled

# No. 55

## Across

**1.** Billiard hall item
**5.** Goon squad member
**9.** Be blasphemous
**14.** Harriet's husband on classic TV
**15.** City of southeastern Kansas
**16.** Artist ___ de Toulouse-Lautrec
**17.** Dairy product uses a rod and lure?
**20.** Amplifier of radio signals
**21.** A graceful ending?
**22.** Act like
**23.** Actor Butterfield of 'Hugo'
**25.** End-of-Ramadan holiday
**26.** Accepted the nomination, say
**27.** Style of New York's Sony Building
**33.** Dad, in Korean
**34.** A short amt. of time
**35.** Gloppy substance
**37.** Blue, say: Abbr
**38.** Biblical witch's home
**41.** B.A. or M.A. offerer
**43.** Angled annexes
**45.** Old musical high note
**46.** Baseball's ___ Gaston
**47.** Lazy
**51.** Banned aerosol propellant, for short
**53.** Adjective after 'red' or 'white'
**54.** "Alice" character
**55.** Amazed person's interjection
**56.** Baseman Melvin
**58.** Bilingual Muppet
**63.** Conceitedly dogmatic
**66.** Feed a line to again
**67.** Frequent recipe words
**68.** Truth, in Toledo
**69.** 'For goodness ___!'
**70.** Avoided honesty
**71.** Byzantine and British, for two: Abbr

## Down

**1.** Gen. ___ E. Lee
**2.** Bleu hue
**3.** Amex competitor
**4.** Certain high-fat, low-carb diet, informally
**5.** Awfully dull
**6.** Cooperstown inst
**7.** Max's secretary in "The Producers"
**8.** Portmanteau coinage for a queer-identified e-sports player, say
**9.** Bash
**10.** Actor Studi
**11.** Having the same pitch but written differently, in a score
**12.** Colombian street food item
**13.** Above the horizon
**18.** A mild cheese
**19.** Ireland's Sinn ___
**24.** Certain game point
**27.** A mouse moves over it
**28.** Andy Taylor's boy
**29.** Computer help for a witch?
**30.** Marvin Gaye's record label
**31.** Bankrupted
**32.** Sans ___
**36.** Bread at a Greek restaurant
**39.** Any of five Norwegian kings
**40.** Brakeman's employer
**42.** A to B, say: Abbr
**44.** Yiddish jerks
**48.** Former Surgeon General C. Everett
**49.** Kind of fibrillation
**50.** Any day
**51.** 'As cold as the Rockies' sloganeer
**52.** Best vision spot
**57.** Beatles song '___ Love Her'
**59.** Act the pack rat
**60.** Account entry
**61.** Boomer Esiason, in college
**62.** Accepts a friend request from
**64.** 'And all too soon, I fear, the king shall ___': 'Richard II'
**65.** Add-on for "rings" or "roads"

# No. 56

## Across

**1.** Dried seaweed popular in Japanese cuisine
**6.** Ballplayer's plug
**10.** Apt rhyme for 'crude' and 'rude'
**14.** A computer hacker usually uses this
**15.** Cyborg's beginning?
**16.** Ancient Greek birthplace of Parmenides
**17.** Noodle count in one of Arizona's largest cities?
**20.** Aerate the soil
**21.** Academic climber
**22.** Brownies and Instamatics
**23.** Duplicate specimen, in biology
**26.** Archaeologists often find what they're looking for in this
**27.** People who maintain golf courses
**32.** Ben of 'Pippin'
**34.** A U.S. senator's is six years
**35.** Entrance to the Medit.
**36.** Bitter brews, for short
**37.** A son of Abe Lincoln
**38.** Alternative to Kodak or Fuji
**39.** Appetizer bowlful
**40.** A first for Arabia?
**42.** Underhanded one
**44.** Guilty pleasure?
**47.** Amuse to the max
**48.** Tempers
**51.** Cluster of mountains
**54.** Abbr. in an auction catalog
**55.** 'Am I talking ___ wall?'
**56.** Result of a merger between Hasbro and Nikon?
**60.** Massive wild ox
**61.** Big model
**62.** Abraham's wife
**63.** Building manager, briefly
**64.** Accessories for suits
**65.** Alternating current pioneer

## Down

**1.** Blues singer McDonald
**2.** Bars from the refrigerator
**3.** Reproductive system?
**4.** Certain Protestant: Abbr.
**5.** Applicability
**6.** Chickenhearted
**7.** Comfortable, as accommodations
**8.** A Mount Rushmore neighbor of Teddy
**9.** More askew
**10.** Precede (with "to")
**11.** A famous Fitzgerald
**12.** Bandleader Lawrence
**13.** Biblical time of rest
**18.** Achieve peak flavor
**19.** Animal emblem
**24.** Andean peak ___ Cruces
**25.** Cry before 'haw'
**26.** Agenda, for short
**28.** Aides, collectively
**29.** Ones whipping things up in the kitchen?
**30.** Abounding
**31.** Keyboard feature
**32.** YouTube clips, briefly
**33.** A grand film
**37.** Almost imperceptible
**38.** Accomplice of sorts
**40.** Avoid the line?
**41.** Business flier
**42.** Eastern takeout meal
**43.** Appear in print
**45.** Calm the nerves of
**46.** Allergic reactions
**49.** Big maker of communications satellites
**50.** A daughter of Barack
**51.** Board events: Abbr.
**52.** "Like Water for Chocolate" director Alfonso
**53.** Added power, in slang
**54.** 'A Series of Unfortunate Events' villainess
**57.** Beatles label, once
**58.** Cologne compass point
**59.** American inventor's monogram

# No. 57

## Across

1. Kemo ___
5. Akin to skin?
11. Agcy. whose future is up in the air?
14. Faithful, in old poetry
15. Be essential (to)
16. Arabic for 'son of'
17. 'Godspeed, Bruno!'
19. Ablaze
20. Anatomical backs
21. Arctic residents
22. Supermarket chain
23. Composer whose name is one letter off from an international peace grp
25. Equip with weapons, old-style
27. Person that's pointed at
32. Former Swedish P.M. Palme
33. Applesauce, essentially
34. Abyssinian's sound
38. A famous one was issued at Nantes
41. A way to rupture
42. 'Bad apple' or 'big cheese'
44. Actor Hemsworth of 'The Hunger Games'
46. Ara
51. Harry Potter's girlfriend
52. Arouse affection
55. Took a course?
57. Cousin of a lemming
60. Felt sun hat
61. 'Homegoing' author Gyasi
62. They appreciate a nice bouquet
64. A question of self-examination
65. A.P. Latin reading
66. Buster Brown's bulldog
67. Daughter of Loki
68. Art form in the Vatican's Raphael Rooms
69. Old English letters

## Down

1. Glam band with six #1 hits in Britain
2. Office chair from Herman Miller
3. Amount of fun, maybe
4. Another name for Dido
5. Alternative to a spinner
6. A loop doesn't have any
7. Actress Perlman
8. Fabled ocean creatures
9. Having the trajectory of a pop-up hit
10. Accessory that might attract bees
11. Big Whig
12. Put ___ on (go for at auction)
13. A demonstrated position?
18. In ___ (isolated)
22. Concert pianist Rubinstein
24. Act amorously
26. Adder relative
28. A coal shuttle
29. Newswoman Gwen
30. Fivescore yrs.
31. Like a double-decker checker
34. Cropped photo?
35. Actor Kier of 'Dancer in the Dark'
36. Raccoon's cousin
37. Actress Perez
39. Actual employer of some 'government consultants,' in brief
40. Actor Larenz
43. Abbr. in cartography
45. After-dinner candies
47. Green-eyed person
48. 'Russian Doll' star Natasha
49. 'Black Swan' role
50. Calypso, e.g.
53. Cartoon cry of consternation
54. Behaves like a souffle
55. Hindu nursemaid
56. Barely risqué
58. Alternative to Levi's
59. Suffix with "diet"
62. Auxiliary service member, once
63. Agitation

# No. 58

## Across

**1.** Apt rhyme for "lewd"
**5.** Clifton of 'Laura'
**9.** Cuckoo ____
**14.** Alternatives to mules
**15.** Financier Kreuger called the Match King
**16.** Sage of India
**17.** Absurd talk
**18.** Basic monetary unit of Ghana
**19.** Gravelly glacial ridge
**20.** Fried-chicken coating
**23.** Adriatic repub
**24.** Outdoor shindigs
**25.** Animal that has escaped from its owner
**27.** Business mogul
**30.** Artery-widening procedure, for short
**32.** Affirmative in 'Fargo'
**33.** Like many a whisper
**37.** Start of a quip about putting things off
**41.** Bump into
**42.** Ad ____ (at the place: Abbr.)
**43.** Ancient symbols of life
**44.** 'Fiddler on the Roof' is set in one
**47.** Extremely harsh
**50.** 'Away!'
**51.** Alley-oop starter
**52.** Home of the Tate Gallery
**58.** Actress Verdugo
**60.** Actor Corey ____
**61.** Aching
**62.** Boy's name that means 'the king'
**63.** Barley-shaped pasta
**64.** Aussie boots
**65.** Adds to a blog
**66.** Back end of a hammer
**67.** A Webmaster may approve it

## Down

**1.** Eddard Stark's heir on 'Game of Thrones'
**2.** Portia to Brutus, e.g.
**3.** Both dis and dat
**4.** Bathe in a glow
**5.** Believer in the Horned God
**6.** Brooklyn's Medgar ____ College
**7.** 'Bag Lady' singer Erykah
**8.** A beanie doesn't have one
**9.** Bygone Toyota sedan
**10.** Easter bloom, in Évreux
**11.** Actor Werner
**12.** Crab's claw
**13.** Pink Nintendo title character
**21.** Abbott and Costello, e.g
**22.** Commenced
**26.** 'Hop ____!'
**27.** A or O, at a blood bank
**28.** A knitter might have a ball with it
**29.** Bonbon, to a Brit
**30.** Adds to the kitty
**31.** Brand of hair remover
**33.** Canal locale: Abbr.
**34.** Acrimony
**35.** Backwards tool?
**36.** Abbr. at the bottom of a letter
**38.** Actor Goran Visnjic, for one
**39.** Missing persons
**40.** A high-top covers it
**44.** Israel's Peres
**45.** Abbr. before a judge's name
**46.** Difficult-to-predict outcome
**47.** Audibly censor
**48.** Hippo on "Captain Kangaroo"
**49.** Airport vehicles
**50.** Smile with one's eyes, per a modern coinage
**53.** Alternative to home ec
**54.** Allowance for weight
**55.** African nation east of Ghana
**56.** Basic work units
**57.** A little shuteye
**59.** Able leader?

# No. 59

## Across

1. Alveoli, bursae, etc.
5. Former steel giant
10. A.B.A. member: Abbr.
14. Actor O'Shea
15. Gave one's parole
16. Das ___ Testament
17. Tallowy
19. Airport fleet
20. Any Club Med
21. Lapful, maybe
23. Handel oratorio
25. Base of Asti wine
26. Bit of advertising
29. A Coen brother
33. Bashed, Biblically
37. Wall: Fr
38. Act the chauffeur
39. Glassmaker's oven
40. A sib
41. 'A Clockwork Orange' hooligan
42. Intestinal
44. Ian Frazier book 'On the ___'
45. 'It's ___ cause'
46. Artist's tools
47. Former inmate
49. A degree
51. Lining material
56. Bash a bug repellent brand?
61. Catches a glimpse of
62. Eye, in Essen
63. Playmakers?
65. Act the worrywart
66. Best Supporting Actor nominee for 'Argo'
67. Accommodate, as passengers
68. A.T.F. agents, e.g
69. Denounces strongly
70. Accused spy Alger

## Down

1. Affected earnestness
2. Actress Anouk
3. Air traveler's choice
4. "American Idol" numbers
5. Aang or Korra
6. Bucharest's home: Abbr.
7. Air kiss sound
8. Sea goddess who was the mother of the Gorgons
9. Classical performance hall
10. Hereditary
11. Japanese audio equipment maker
12. Band's big brass
13. Recently: Abbr.
18. Act curmudgeonly
22. Accused of infringement, say
24. Dude, in Durango
27. Dye-producing gastropod
28. Painter whose 'Zapatistas' is on display at MoMA
30. Aloha State city
31. Ancient greetings
32. Adjacent
33. Big loser's nickname?
34. He, for one: Abbr
35. Expressed surprise
36. They may come with bells and whistles
43. Carrie Chapman ___
45. Acute feeling of anxiety
48. Aphrodite's accompaniers
50. Amateur on a board
52. Copycatting
53. A child of Japanese immigrants
54. Greek Zs
55. Aides: Abbr
56. Course clinker
57. A fly is a common one
58. Acquired wisdom, per a saying
59. Arizona's Agua ___ National Monument
60. Barn's place
64. About half of all adults

# No. 60

## Across

**1.** Software creators, for short
**5.** Actress Graynor
**8.** 'American Idol' contestant Felton
**13.** A CFO is one
**14.** Bach's '___, Joy of Man's Desiring'
**16.** Cheri formerly of 'S.N.L'
**17.** Fashion house known for its paisley patterns
**18.** Esau's first wife
**19.** Arbor
**20.** Reporters who were trained in Washington, D.C.?
**23.** Bluish-gray in color
**24.** Another Tolkien creature
**25.** Bairn-sized
**28.** Something followed at school
**33.** Actor Danson
**36.** 'Am I talking ___ wall?'
**37.** Auxiliary propositions, in math
**38.** In a real mess
**41.** Examine by touching
**42.** 'Bueller?'
**43.** Average of tre and nove
**44.** Casting call shout
**45.** New product line after USPS's takeover of Firestone?
**49.** 'Aaron Burr, ___'
**50.** A wool producer
**51.** App whose icon features a camera, in slang
**55.** Gates and Jobs, e.g.
**60.** Acapulco beach
**62.** 'A likely story'
**63.** Anecdotal collections
**64.** Cheap so-and-so
**65.** Bath swell
**66.** Cable-___ sweater
**67.** 'Chocolat' director Hallstroem
**68.** Big inits. in electronic games
**69.** Absolution targets

## Down

**1.** Areas explored by submarines
**2.** Commend highly
**3.** Compact Nissan model
**4.** Operatic baritone Antonio
**5.** A bit cracked
**6.** Hawthorne novel stigma
**7.** Dance pioneer Duncan
**8.** Gen. ___ E. Lee
**9.** Ally of the Missouri, once
**10.** Murphy Brown was one
**11.** Andre Young a.k.a. Dr. ___
**12.** An empty bottle is full of it
**15.** African political movement
**21.** OB/___
**22.** Cheers
**26.** A maternal relation
**27.** Anglo-Saxon kingdom
**29.** Conn man
**30.** Beatrix Potter's 'The Tale of Mr. ___'
**31.** Abbr. before a number
**32.** Accusing of misconduct
**33.** Alexander and others
**34.** 'Been there, done that' feeling
**35.** Dawns
**39.** Certain pocket-watch retainer
**40.** A in French
**41.** Aloo matar morsel
**43.** Child by marriage
**46.** A gym rat may break one
**47.** A.T.M. need
**48.** Devious ones
**52.** Alternative to Shiite
**53.** Amtrak service
**54.** Aides: Abbr
**56.** Actress Carrie and others
**57.** Allowance for weight
**58.** Abounding
**59.** Bad grades
**60.** Individuals, for short
**61.** Debussy's 'Air de ___'

# No. 61

## Across

**1.** Adz, e.g

**5.** Bantu-speaking people of Rwanda

**9.** Beer brand often mentioned in country music

**14.** Bean pot

**15.** Actor Ken

**16.** Alps-to-Arles river

**17.** Alpine native

**20.** Find a definition for

**21.** Adequately, to Li'l Abner

**22.** A barber has to work around it

**23.** Atlantic state in two time zones: Abbr.

**25.** A Santa in California

**26.** Actress Wilson of 'Mrs. Doubtfire'

**27.** Tireless in pursuit of weight control?

**33.** Absolute must

**34.** Beatrix Potter's 'The Tale of Mr. ___'

**35.** Dark Lord of the ___ ('Star Wars' title)

**37.** Bait fish

**38.** Academy of arms equipment

**41.** A bit smashed?

**43.** Aladdin's discovery

**45.** Alex and ___ (jewelry brand)

**46.** Tiber tributary whose name means 'black'

**47.** GEAR, geometrically

**51.** Asian affirmative

**53.** A service winner

**54.** A primary color

**55.** 'A jealous mistress,' per Emerson

**56.** German pop star who once had a #2 song

**58.** Cancel out

**63.** Jigger

**66.** Actress Holmes

**67.** Ahi specification

**68.** Bygone Chevrolet

**69.** Arab, maybe

**70.** Like many a PAC

**71.** Alternative to nuts?

## Down

**1.** Additional-axle charge

**2.** A bit of this, a bit of that

**3.** Alternate for butter

**4.** Absence

**5.** Dorm room appliance

**6.** Cousin of -kin or -let

**7.** Antler branch

**8.** Detangle

**9.** Quick-to-erect homes

**10.** Bigeye or yellowfin tuna

**11.** Job mistakenly sought by a dominoes champ?

**12.** Act furtively

**13.** Absorbent cloth

**18.** Angry, resentful state

**19.** A sandwich filler

**24.** At the acme

**27.** Alternative to Dem. and Rep

**28.** Actor McDonough

**29.** Head off?

**30.** A plant disease

**31.** Absolutely perfect

**32.** Chinese weight unit

**36.** Bar mitzvah dance

**39.** Cabinet dept. with a sun on its seal

**40.** Issued a gag order on

**42.** Candy treat

**44.** Moved like a show horse

**48.** Banda ___ (2004 Indonesian tsunami site)

**49.** Mark who played Spock's father

**50.** Ancient concert halls

**51.** Birds associated with war

**52.** Buddhist in nirvana

**57.** Amo follower

**59.** Bag handle?

**60.** An inventor's middle name

**61.** A bride and groom may be on the top one

**62.** A footbridge from Windsor leads to it

**64.** A shootout might end it

**65.** A form of "to be"

# No. 62

## Across

**1.** Academy offering
**6.** Blue material?
**10.** Adjective for the Road Runner
**14.** Antisocial type
**15.** Assistant played by Bruce Lee
**16.** Welcome, as a visitor / Try to make a date with
**17.** Job for one doing character studies?
**20.** A giant among Giants
**21.** Do, re or mi, in Italy
**22.** Alternative to J.F.K. and La Guardia
**23.** Laced waterproof boot
**26.** 'A Song of Ice and Fire,' e.g
**27.** Sales techniques
**32.** Ark site after the conquest of Canaan
**34.** Angry chorus
**35.** Aught
**36.** Gumshoes, in old crime fiction
**37.** Barbecue discard
**38.** Actor awarded a Distinguished Flying Cross in W.W. II
**39.** Actress Thurman
**40.** Prophet in the Book of Mormon
**42.** Apparel item
**44.** Taking one's sweet time
**47.** 'A God in Ruins' novelist
**48.** Act of deletion
**51.** Hand in
**54.** Cardio : heart :: ___ : ear
**55.** Antietam fighter (Abbr.)
**56.** Discuss by phone
**60.** Asian capital name starter
**61.** Benefit from planting
**62.** Agricultural apparatus
**63.** Action in FanDuel and DraftKings
**64.** Address for multiple knights
**65.** Altered tones?

## Down

**1.** Adele and Cher, e.g
**2.** 'Antiques Roadshow' determination
**3.** Relating to structure, in a way
**4.** Animated chihuahua
**5.** A.M.A. members: Abbr.
**6.** Bandleader Henderson
**7.** First name in espionage
**8.** Adaptable truck, for short
**9.** Alley ___
**10.** Decrees from mullahs
**11.** About a third of all land
**12.** Candy bar with a crown logo
**13.** 'Peter Pan' fairy, for short
**18.** Aquarium bottom-feeder
**19.** Athena's shield
**24.** Adult elvers
**25.** Active leader?
**26.** Arrogant one
**28.** A watched pot is never this
**29.** Office addresses?
**30.** Ballpoint points
**31.** Adhesive for false eyelashes
**32.** Alternative to draw or hold 'em
**33.** Engine option
**37.** Addams who created the Addams family
**38.** About half of all deliveries
**40.** A mondegreen is a misheard one
**41.** Cosmopolitan group
**42.** Childe Harold's creator
**43.** Debussy's 'Air de ___'
**45.** Bulb units
**46.** Abatements
**49.** Action after a bad golf drive
**50.** "At the Movies" name
**51.** Admission evidence
**52.** One of two rivers forming the Ubangi
**53.** Baa relative
**54.** 'A jug of wine . . .' poet Khayyam
**57.** 'Don't tell ___ can't ...!'
**58.** Author Chinua Achebe, by birth
**59.** A dance, when doubled

# No. 63

## Across

**1.** Bronze coin in the Harry Potter books
**5.** Brilliantly colored flower
**11.** Agitated, with 'up'
**14.** Add-on for "million"
**15.** Heap
**16.** Alternative to Gain
**17.** Northern European region
**19.** Atlantis docked with it
**20.** Fox hunt cry
**21.** California's Santa ___ Mountains
**22.** Abominable Snowman
**23.** Cheerios, abroad
**25.** Ancient Greek wear
**27.** Harassment with a mouse
**32.** Aid for catching a mouse
**33.** Belly bulge
**34.** Sea lettuce
**38.** Bob who pitched for both the Mets and Yankees
**41.** Actual wording
**42.** Abandon détente
**44.** 'Nothing beats ___' (beer slogan)
**46.** Some obfuscating jargon
**51.** Battle locale that marked a turning point in W.W. I
**52.** Big laugh
**55.** Abbott, to Costello, e.g.
**57.** Asian monk
**60.** Old newspaper photo sections, informally
**61.** Actor Chaney
**62.** Hard heads?
**64.** Abbr. for the most extreme
**65.** Colorless ketone
**66.** Another graceful seabird
**67.** Basic college degrees
**68.** Aeronautics pioneer Clyde
**69.** Alphabetizing, e.g.: Abbr

## Down

**1.** Buckwheat bowlful
**2.** Certain dry cell, briefly
**3.** Language family that includes Finnish and Hungarian
**4.** Two-time world skating champ Albright
**5.** 'Amarillo' chili pepper
**6.** Clownish
**7.** A.A. Milne's first name
**8.** 'Cowboy Man' singer Lyle
**9.** External parasites
**10.** Actress Cash of FX's "You're the Worst"
**11.** It's a lot
**12.** Ballpark stadium sign
**13.** A famous Amos
**18.** 'But what if I'm wrong?' feeling
**22.** Native of eastern Siberia
**24.** Dry, in combinations
**26.** Day follower?
**28.** British rule in colonial India
**29.** Aborigine's weapon
**30.** Counterorder
**31.** Avenge oneself on
**34.** City area, briefly
**35.** Basic unit of Romanian currency
**36.** Troublesome critters
**37.** "He's ___ nowhere man"
**39.** Abbr. before a trade name
**40.** Bibliog. info
**43.** Bang up, e.g
**45.** Beloved ones
**47.** Loosen, as a corset
**48.** Brings to a halt
**49.** Young hogs (var.)
**50.** Automat, e.g.
**53.** Band section
**54.** A keen eye, for a proofreader, say
**55.** Bit for the blooper reel
**56.** Alley's girlfriend
**58.** N.Y.S.E. and Nasdaq, e.g.
**59.** A king of Judah
**62.** Center X or O
**63.** A near-Miss. state

## Across

1. Alta's opposite
5. Acute onset
9. Arthropod appendages
14. Certain Dadaist works
15. Medieval chest
16. Ancient assembly area
17. Again
18. At one's ___ and call
19. 'Born ___'
20. Diet, e.g
23. Also say
24. Bewailed
25. Banded cameo stones
27. Bible book with the most verses
30. Ape Hans Brinker
32. Brief summer month?
33. Atlas index listing
37. Wanted: ordinary haberdasher
41. Cause for budget cutting
42. Ad or show follower
43. Brings into balance
44. 'American ___' (Gere movie)
47. Famed insurer
50. Base of a window
51. Kobe Bryant's team, on scoreboards
52. Miserly ones
58. The Bahamas' Great ___ Island
60. Ancient one
61. Archaic auxiliary
62. Big fancy house
63. Beginning to type?
64. Fats Domino's 'It's ___ Love'
65. Actor Braugher
66. Acts as a quizmaster
67. Alternative to whole

## Down

1. A false god
2. 'A-Hunting We Will Go' composer
3. Compressed file format
4. Eddying
5. Dark cousins of weasels
6. Bald tire's lack
7. A debit card is linked to one: Abbr
8. Asian oil capital
9. Inventor, at times
10. A long time ___
11. Critic of the Once-ler, with 'the'
12. Fuddy-duddy
13. Beach blankets?
21. Abacus calculation
22. Blunt end?
26. Aching desires
27. A bear encountered by Goldilocks
28. Bridge worker of TV
29. Bygone dignitaries
30. Airtimes
31. 'A maid with hair of gold,' in an old song
33. Ballerina's bend
34. Church stand
35. A lot of it is junk
36. Auto designer Ferrari
38. Eensy-weensy
39. Music genre that includes 'geeksta rap'
40. Compact cars?
44. Beanie propellers and such: Var.
45. Breed
46. Knight from Atlanta
47. Alpaca kin
48. Brother of Rebecca, in the Bible
49. Chan portrayer
50. Feistiness or courage
53. Faulkner character ___ Varner
54. American cuckoos
55. Applied oneself (to)
56. A case of pins and needles
57. Adjust with a wedge
59. Either of two NT books

# No. 65

## Across

**1.** A.C. measures
**5.** Be in need of the Heimlich maneuver
**10.** A large order
**14.** Association
**15.** Afghan or basset
**16.** Spanish tennis star Carlos
**17.** Treeless
**19.** Card game named for an island
**20.** He wrote the best sellers 'Couplehood' and 'Babyhood'
**21.** Came to
**23.** It may have clawed feet
**25.** Adjective for a sack?
**26.** Capital of Nigeria
**29.** Block, old-style
**33.** Bilbo steals from his hoard of treasure
**37.** Bit of code
**38.** Female companion in 'Doctor Who'
**39.** Be the first to use
**40.** Computer printer meas.
**41.** Darkroom images, for short
**42.** Detach by tearing
**44.** Actor who overacts
**45.** Amusement park ride feature
**46.** Pop singer Taylor
**47.** Actor Williams of 'Happy Days'
**49.** A.T.M. transaction: Abbr
**51.** Absence of harmful bacteria
**56.** One without equal
**61.** Italy's ___ alla Scala
**62.** Battler of Hector at Troy
**63.** Highway ramp style
**65.** Act like a lunatic
**66.** Adorable one
**67.** Actress Condor
**68.** Conked out, as an engine
**69.** "A Doll's House" dramatist
**70.** A schussboomer uses them

## Down

**1.** Article teaser
**2.** Athlete's foot
**3.** Dis-qualified?
**4.** Mere smidgen
**5.** Angel child
**6.** Book after Daniel: Abbr.
**7.** Carve ___ niche
**8.** Appreciated
**9.** Classic Icelandic literary works
**10.** Fixed insertion
**11.** A shark might give you one
**12.** Actor MacLachlan
**13.** Aforementioned
**18.** Adjust the price on
**22.** Critic Pauline
**24.** Founder of an Eastern religion
**27.** Akita's land
**28.** Jainist principle
**30.** Anheuser-Busch product
**31.** Aquarium growth
**32.** Abrade with a tool
**33.** Cold War missile type
**34.** Abe Simpson's estranged wife
**35.** Amply ventilated
**36.** Hard to research
**43.** Certain letters of the alphabet
**45.** Arrogant look
**48.** Televangelist Joel
**50.** Emilio of fashion
**52.** 'Back in my day ...'
**53.** A vegan might make it from tofu or cauliflower
**54.** Afghan's neighbor
**55.** Certain convertibles
**56.** Ancient fragrance
**57.** California city north of Ventura
**58.** Apse neighbor
**59.** After-school group
**60.** Attraction, so to speak, with 'the'
**64.** Be a competitor

# No. 66

## Across

1. Agency employee
5. Abbr. for the most extreme
8. Capital of Minorca
13. 'A Day Without Rain' artist
14. Arable soil
16. A long, amateurish piano recital, maybe
17. Antiquated 'not'
18. Attachment to "nautics" or "dynamic"
19. Aspic ___ (savory French dish)
20. Nora Ephron and Sofia Coppola, for two
23. A great composer?
24. Amsterdam of l'Océan Indien, e.g
25. American inventor's monogram
28. Distracting tactics
33. BHO's signature legislation
36. Blood-type abbr.
37. TV producer Don
38. Sack materials
41. Certain plate
42. Astronomer's light ratio
43. Activist Mallory
44. Awacs component: Abbr
45. Bicycle mechanic?
49. Beginning of a laugh
50. A samara source
51. Bit of cuneiform
55. Gates and Jobs, e.g.
60. Aide to Luke
62. Villain's symbol
63. 'Act!'
64. Becomes bitter
65. Airtight tower
66. Big model
67. Choir pieces
68. Animals in un zoológico
69. All roads lead to it, in a saying

## Down

1. All in knots
2. Bring to life onstage
3. A gift of the Magi
4. Check cashers, usually
5. Asian capital name starter
6. Big name in cinemas
7. Drags one's feet
8. Caster of spells
9. 'Ain't She Sweet' composer Milton
10. Black-and-white grazers
11. 'A Chorus Line' number
12. Actress Carrie
15. Works hard, old-style
21. 'Uhh ...'
22. Crash analyzers
26. Champing at the bit
27. Adlai's running mate
29. Anti
30. Belts boxers don't want to receive?
31. A little fun?
32. A wool producer
33. Bring embarrassment to
34. Apology ending
35. Botanical garden
39. Albania currency unit
40. Add-on for Gator
41. Actress ___ Park Lincoln
43. Graceland locale
46. Ancient Roman citizenry
47. 'A Room of One's ___'
48. Destitute person
52. Cathedral of Florence
53. Andersen contemporary
54. Accented perfume bottle name
56. Norse goddess of fate
57. Attempt at a carnival booth
58. Abnormal breathing
59. A footbridge from Windsor leads to it
60. A grate build-up
61. Activist Aruna

# No. 67

## Across

1. Acronymic band name
5. Liter lead-in
9. British college
14. Asian country next to Thailand
15. Actor ___ Ross
16. Badly made dough?
17. One way of ordering things, like all the consonants in rows three, six and nine
20. African antelope or Chevrolet
21. A leading manufacturer of cars
22. A O doesn't have one
23. An eye for poetry?
25. Abbr. on some statements
26. Arca de ___ (boat in la biblia)
27. Temp job?
33. Algerian city
34. Alternative genre
35. Aromatic plant found in some pets
37. Basket and thatch palm
38. Actress Gurira
41. Bit of foppish attire
43. Sergeant in 'The Thin Red Line'
45. Armory item
46. Alps or Appalachians: Abbr
47. Law offices?
51. A.T.M. input: Abbr
53. Celebrity chef Martin
54. Actor Danson
55. Actress ___ Park Lincoln
56. Being with une auréole
58. Airlift, maybe
63. A dull wit
66. A dancing Astaire
67. Author Birkerts
68. 'American Sniper' setting
69. A choir may stand on it
70. Backpack item
71. Climber's rocky spots

## Down

1. Asia's Trans ___ mountains
2. Aloe, naturally
3. Astronomer Thomas for whom a comet is named
4. Author bandele
5. Excluded from a place
6. Actress Lindley
7. Ancient Roman censor
8. Ab ___ (from the beginning)
9. Adaptable
10. Call's opposite
11. Half of the Nobel Prize winners, typically
12. America East Conference town
13. Tribe of the Amistad slaves
18. Another word for 'potato'
19. Cry after a successful insult
24. Capital of the former Belgian Congo
27. Address in Jamaica
28. Actor Estrada
29. The Met's 'Hunt of the Unicorn' and others
30. Bring to life onstage
31. It appears in droves
32. Big name at SeaWorld
36. Accutane target
39. A parental sibling
40. Occurring naturally
42. Bygone covert org.
44. Person with a paddle
48. Hyperbolic function
49. Take into the body
50. Abused an Rx dosage, say
51. A kamidana is a small one
52. Islamic messiah
57. A gutter is often under it
59. Agitated condition
60. Atlantic food fish
61. Companion of the Natl. Guard
62. A.B.A. members' titles
64. A.L. Central city
65. Animal lair

# No. 68

## Across

1. Dollars in Iran
6. Beverages in bowls
10. Asian cookers
14. Austen's 'Northanger ___'
15. Actress ___ Shawkat of 'Arrested Development'
16. A shake in the grass?
17. Deprived of fast food chains?
20. Dye family
21. Adore, cutesily
22. Carroll's mad tea-drinker
23. British dish with an American version called a Hot Brown
26. A stet cancels it
27. Student of fossil plants with scattered money from a shark?
32. Stage when an animal is in heat
34. A reduced amount
35. A voiced vote
36. Dashiell Hammett's 'The ___ Curse'
37. Author of 'The Silent World: A Story of Undersea Discovery and Adventure'
38. Korean autos
39. Actor Tognazzi
40. Christine ___, heroine of 'The Phantom of the Opera'
42. A star in France
44. Long-running TV show featuring match-makers
47. Barley beards
48. Alley's edges
51. Guinea-___
54. A. E. Housman's 'A Shropshire ___'
55. "Applesauce!"
56. Contrary to the rules
60. Abrasion aftermath
61. Aboard a liner
62. Accented perfume bottle name
63. Beginning to flop?
64. Aids in storming castle gates
65. Andrea Gibson works

## Down

1. Aid in detecting speeders
2. Island famous for its nightlife
3. Bounty work?
4. Abstract artist Krasner
5. Abridged, for short: Abbr.
6. Best-selling Japanese manga series
7. A king of Norway
8. Alcohol that's transparent
9. Drawer fresheners
10. Bleach
11. Apt anagram of 'outs'
12. 'Ad Parnassum' painter
13. Abolhassan Bani-___ (first president of Iran)
18. Airborne distractions
19. Chicago Bears coaching legend George
24. Achieve through hard work
25. Bassist DeTiger
26. Accomplishes
28. More depressed
29. Burn to a crisp
30. Attack, with 'into'
31. Chinook salmon
32. Another cabinet dept
33. A powdery starch
37. Beanies, berets, etc
38. Annoyance for Santa
40. Big name in scotch
41. O-shaped
42. Bit of music at a music conservatory
43. A little birdie
45. Bright yellow fruit
46. Brightly colored lizards
49. 'Air Music' composer
50. Afflictions known technically as hordeola
51. Abject failure
52. Director Thomas H. ___ of the silent era
53. Airplane wing supporter
54. Mostly bygone airline amenity
57. 'Beauty ___ Witch' (Shakespeare poem)
58. Brady bunch, in headlines
59. Chicken general

# No. 69

## Across

1. At ___ speed (quickly)
5. Agita
11. Bird beak
14. Scrooge's fault
15. Move in an ungainly way
16. A mean Amin
17. Big leagues
19. Advertising icon Elsie, e.g
20. Actress Van Devere
21. Armory holdings
22. Tony Musante TV series
23. Alphabetization, for one
25. Boundary
27. Instruction for a future congressperson?
32. British term for a row of houses converted from stables
33. Actress Roberts
34. Abates, as a tide
38. Bring to an end
41. Barely communicate?
42. Abrupt transitions
44. Chuck ___, four-time Super Bowl-winning coach
46. Predatory wasps
51. Andrew Cuomo's father
52. A tremendous supply
55. A straight cut
57. Long-distance swimmer Diana
60. A bad one should be kicked
61. Activist Mallory
62. Thoughtful
64. A mammal has three
65. Big name in flatware
66. Abandoned garden
67. Alcohol-friendly
68. Big maker of GPS devices
69. Stella ___ (biscuit brand)

## Down

1. Conveys lightly
2. Actor James of 'The Fresh Prince of Bel-Air'
3. Base for many a chef's rose garnish
4. Abracadabra alternative
5. Ending with form
6. The 'N' of N.B
7. Kind of round in a tournament, informally
8. Gold Glove winner Roberto
9. Another California wine-growing region
10. Baker's dozen for the Beatles, for short
11. Ingredient in some gum
12. Ancient Dead Sea country
13. Japan's largest lake
18. Case of the sniffles
22. Brown and others
24. Approx. camera flash duration
26. Accepted the bait
28. A wool producer
29. Blue Nile source (Var.)
30. Greek goddess of the night
31. B movie shooter
34. Actor Ron who played Tarzan on TV
35. A domesticated insect
36. Most pleasantly warm
37. Accident sound
39. Alternative to Rep. or Dem.
40. City in Nevada
43. Campus Greek grp
45. Bebé's milk
47. A Ryder
48. Fast Florence
49. Got emotional, with 'up'
50. Saturday, in Seville
53. Atacama Desert export
54. Aide with a pad
55. Black-and-white duck
56. Bad, like a 'dad joke'
58. 'Just ___ about to ...'
59. Actress Conn
62. Bit player
63. Actor Aykroyd

## Across

1. Android purchases
5. Dumb goon
9. Bird's attempt at communication
14. Ashram authority
15. Best friend's dinner, maybe
16. Agent Swifty
17. Another name for Cupid
18. Antony's love, briefly
19. Creazione di ___ (Sistine ceiling section)
20. Friday, 'Tabla Solo In Jhaptal'
23. City where Cézanne was born
24. Anti-resistance units?
25. Detachable shirtfront
27. Alpha Canis Majoris
30. Carryout item?
32. A suitor may pitch it
33. Land famed for its cuisine
37. Supporting nativist policies
41. Paint jobs at the back of the airplane?
42. Alfred E. Neuman's magazine
43. Artist Neiman
44. Soundin
47. Californi____ name translates to 'the table'
50. Eminem guested on his song "Smack That"
51. Krupp of the NHL
52. Order of ants
58. Absolutely absurd
60. Ablutionary vessel
61. British philosopher A.J.
62. Something to watch on la télé
63. Bozo
64. Auto finish?
65. Acclimate
66. Achieves with difficulty (With "out")
67. Bagpiper's lids

## Down

1. Actor John of 'Sands of Iwo Jima'
2. Agile predator
3. Can. division
    o imitate
5. Domineering men
6. Clay pots
7. Accepting business
8. Eccentric individual
9. Mrs. Dalloway in 'Mrs. Dalloway'
10. Birthed
11. 'The Compleat Angler' author Walton
12. Easily wrinkled fabric
13. Absentee ballot
21. Chinese dish: moo ___ pork
22. Deborah of 'Days of Our Lives'
26. Debt memo
27. Acronym on a police jacket
28. Burial place of Macbeth
29. Bread eaten with curry
30. Hoity-___
31. Afghans, e.g
33. 'Hahahahahaha!'
34. Aligns the crosshairs
35. Actor Centineo
36. Artist Warhol
38. He: Lat
39. Antarctic mass
40. Conger cousin
44. Cousins of culottes
45. 'Doo ___ (That Thing)' (#1 hit for Lauryn Hill)
46. All there
47. Miller of opera
48. Bearded, as grain
49. Actress Anne with four Emmy nominations
50. Anoint
53. Ancient Assyrian foe
54. Arboreal sci-fi creature
55. South American wildcat
56. Amount of paper
57. A&E word
59. A small drink

# No. 71

## Across

1. Antifreeze?
5. Arm joint
10. Balls in the sky
14. Frog genus that's Spanish for 'frog'
15. Back biter
16. Botanical trunk
17. Foreglimpse
19. Cocksure
20. Agemate
21. Goes to pieces?
23. Turbulence caused by conflicting currents
25. Flooey lead-in
26. Coin of Kolkata
29. A boring person might have one
33. Barbecues badly
37. Andalusian article
38. Achieve one's goal?
39. Easily handled, as a ship
40. Appropriate rhyme for 'spa'
41. Actions on heartstrings and pant legs
42. Boards up
44. Abe's birthday mo
45. Ban legally
46. 'Officially Missing You' artist
47. Alluring skirt features
49. Combined with
51. Eavesdropping on the most conversations, maybe
56. Bane of elitists
61. Changer of skins into leather
62. Actor Julia
63. Iridescent quality of some gems
65. Amala de Xango vegetable
66. Appear at intervals
67. Brief shots?
68. A sometimes-blonde, e.g.
69. New York city near Binghamton
70. Barfly's binge

## Down

1. Area for development
2. An Asian capital
3. Bought in
4. Choose to forfeit
5. Actress Clarke of 'Game of Thrones'
6. Amputate (with "off")
7. 'Gil ___'
8. Bit of salty language
9. AC/DC single with the lyric 'watch me explode'
10. Plugs up
11. All roads lead to it, in a saying
12. Astigmatic view
13. Pts. of a line
18. Acts the nitpicker
22. Affairs that might sate the British
24. Rice dishes
27. African region including Khartoum and Timbuktu
28. Cinder holder
30. Affliction of Benjamin Franklin
31. Accordingly
32. Court defendant: Abbr
33. Abnormal body sac
34. 'So funny!'
35. Boxing promoter Bob
36. Netlike
43. AMC's 'Better Call ___'
45. 'A Modest Proposal,' e.g.
48. 'My Neighbor ___' (Studio Ghibli film)
50. Brewery opening?
52. Hardly suitable
53. Cinematic scorer Morricone
54. Painting on dry plaster
55. A private eye might videotape one
56. Bit of elbow encouragement
57. Barrel-flavored, as wine
58. Chaste
59. Ed Sullivan's "really big ___"
60. Airborne defense?
64. Attention-getting pull

# No. 72

## Across

**1.** Ashram authority
**5.** Infrequent: Abbr.
**8.** Accept formally
**13.** Amenhotep IV's god
**14.** Backup cause
**16.** Dust sprinkler of folklore
**17.** Moistens flax
**18.** Additional-axle charge
**19.** Tradesman, e.g
**20.** Like some cruises
**23.** Goddesses guarding the gates of Olympus
**24.** George Harrison's '___ Mine'
**25.** Animal in un zoológico
**28.** What were Russell and Anna Huxtable on 'The Cosby Show'?
**33.** Act as if
**36.** A raised hand might indicate it
**37.** Cowboy ropes
**38.** Lacking serviceability
**41.** Igneous rock
**42.** Andre of tennis fame
**43.** Animated chihuahua
**44.** A new beginning?
**45.** Cookout option for someone avoiding red meat
**49.** Actor Butterfield of 'Hugo'
**50.** Academy Award winner for 'Moonlight' and 'Green Book'
**51.** Bring to an end
**55.** Negative fast-food review?
**60.** Alternative to Travelers
**62.** Ancient Greek earth goddess
**63.** Carve ___ niche
**64.** Air condition?
**65.** Blogger's code
**66.** Granite paving block
**67.** Gland prefix
**68.** Abbr. in an auction catalog
**69.** A gas from the past

## Down

**1.** Brooks from Tulsa
**2.** Developing, after "in"
**3.** Cover again, as a road
**4.** Detangle
**5.** Eight, as a prefix
**6.** Aneurysm cause
**7.** Disagree sharply
**8.** Abbr. on a doctor's schedule
**9.** Capital and largest city of East Timor
**10.** Percocet relative
**11.** A wedge might come out of it
**12.** Artist Gerard ___ Borch
**15.** Stay outdoors overnight with some of the comforts of home
**21.** Address from a rev.
**22.** Getting warm, so to speak
**26.** A star may represent it
**27.** Bone head?
**29.** Pop star who starred in 'Queen of the Damned'
**30.** Actress Carrie
**31.** 'A Rainy Night in ___' (1946 hit)
**32.** A barber has to work around it
**33.** Cowboy's lasso
**34.** Beef cattle breed
**35.** Bold promise
**39.** Admonisher's sound
**40.** Advert's ending?
**41.** Aachen article
**43.** Cause to fall
**46.** Bounty name
**47.** Antique coin
**48.** Ascended again
**52.** Bouts of chills
**53.** Paving stones
**54.** A sister of Calliope
**56.** Act ___ impulse
**57.** Arum family member
**58.** Birthstones, e.g
**59.** Estonian or Lithuanian
**60.** BHO's signature legislation
**61.** Ancient times, in ancient times

# No. 73

## Across

1. Apple of Discord goddess
5. Minute amount
9. Deeply piled
14. A lot of volume?
15. 'Aladdin' character named after a literary villain
16. Bunch of, casually
17. What a poor diet may need
20. Lead-in to day or year
21. Caviars
22. City in central Israel
23. Animals in un zoológico
25. A few bucks at Pimlico
26. Admission requirements, perhaps
27. Ape suit wearer?
33. Area near Little Italy
34. Baby newt
35. Dutch landscapist Aelbert ____
37. Barnyard outbursts
38. Grassy surface
41. Everyone included, after 'to'
43. 'A Life for the ____' (Mikhail Glinka opera)
45. A little bull
46. Avoid uniformity
47. Astrology or palmistry
51. A patient response?
53. Abbr. on a toothpaste box
54. Bacon, familiarly
55. Amnesty International, e.g., in brief
56. Acquires, informally
58. Hawaii's Forbidden Isle
63. Likely to change everything
66. Bring a smile to
67. Accomplish flawlessly
68. Administered by mouth
69. Abrasive files
70. Like a flan
71. A bit too interested

## Down

1. Artsy-craftsy website
2. Cad, rake or bounder
3. Baby sitter's handfuls
4. A third of vingt-et-un
5. Diphthong dividers
6. Animal in a flock
7. Bob ____, longtime Disney C.E.O
8. Chimpanzee variety
9. Alternative to paper
10. Alitalia : Italy :: ____ : Poland
11. Flexible baseball player
12. Acknowledged an anthem
13. Analog clock features
18. Injured: Fr
19. Adolescent
24. 'Avoid watching this at the office,' briefly
27. Alcohol chaser?
28. Academic, as an arguable point
29. Element in some match heads
30. Día de San Valentín bouquet
31. Aviator ____ Balbo
32. Almost too smooth
36. Bois de Boulogne, par exemple
39. Actuary's calculation
40. In a respectable way
42. Actress Carrie
44. Gets as far as
48. Japanese salad plants
49. English novelist du Maurier
50. Ellington band vocalist Anderson
51. At hand, in poems
52. Blue-headed lizard
57. Food eaten during Lohri
59. A heavy metal
60. Director Murai
61. Anecdotal collections
62. Beyond homely
64. A small dose: Abbr.
65. 'Boyish Girl Interrupted' comedian Notaro

# No. 74

## Across

**1.** Locales of many work-related injuries
**6.** Army command
**10.** Ball team wear
**14.** Prayer ending
**15.** Bones in the pelvic area
**16.** Activewear brand
**17.** Extreme exposure
**20.** Actor Benicio ___ Toro
**21.** A little or a lot
**22.** Distinct periods of history
**23.** Basil's cousin
**26.** Either separately ___ combination
**27.** Like Merriam-Webster's inclusion of the word 'irregardless,' originally
**32.** Baja California, por ejemplo
**34.** Broad
**35.** A hot one can burn you
**36.** Act the butterfly
**37.** Air or field starter
**38.** Asked for a ticket, in a way
**39.** Erev ___ (Hebrew good evening)
**40.** A cygnet is a baby one
**42.** Ancient assembly sites
**44.** A rung on the ladder of life
**47.** Author Jaffe
**48.** 'Le Rhinocéros' playwright
**51.** B westerns
**54.** Acrimonious
**55.** 'Be there in a ___!'
**56.** Sasquatch studier, say
**60.** Akbar's capital
**61.** A lion has one
**62.** Astronomers' sightings
**63.** A dobbin might pull one
**64.** Achieved laboriously (with "out")
**65.** Certainly not disguised

## Down

**1.** Red River tribe
**2.** Arab chieftain
**3.** Like a mirror
**4.** April second?
**5.** A home away from home
**6.** Certain claimant
**7.** 'For Better or for Worse' matriarch
**8.** 'A pox on you!'
**9.** Incapacitated temporarily, in a way
**10.** Bodies of rules
**11.** Accompanying, in Avignon
**12.** Disdainful remark
**13.** Act the wisenheimer
**18.** Antônio, for one
**19.** A church could have one
**24.** A kid is a young one
**25.** A 'little word' in charades
**26.** 'Amores' poet
**28.** Because of (with "to")
**29.** 'Wow'
**30.** Town in Honolulu County
**31.** Alternatives to plasma TVs
**32.** Baby newts
**33.** A.T.M. feature
**37.** 'Every ___ king'
**38.** Acoustic measure
**40.** Accommodating person
**41.** Appealing in appearance
**42.** Any of the Marshall Islands
**43.** Angled: Suffix
**45.** Compensate in advance
**46.** Like fodder, in the winter
**49.** Activist Chavez
**50.** Assemblage of eight
**51.** Andean tubers
**52.** Frustrated exclamation
**53.** Actress Ferrell
**54.** Actress Skye
**57.** Director/ screenwriter Penn
**58.** A Beatle bride
**59.** Alternative to 'com'

# No. 75

## Across

**1.** A few last words
**5.** Metal sheeting used in aircraft
**11.** Alternative greeting to a high-five
**14.** A driver may change one
**15.** Dean Martin hit
**16.** Aggravate
**17.** Infinitesimal
**19.** Add to threads?
**20.** Arkansas' ___ Mountains
**21.** Actress Miranda
**22.** Last name of London criminal twins Ronnie and Reggie
**23.** Address for a Juárez wife
**25.** Alternate passage, in a score
**27.** Teaches a ceramics class?
**32.** A little dense
**33.** Aspic ___ (savory French dish)
**34.** All-purpose trucks
**38.** Audible kiss
**41.** Actress Diana of "The Avengers"
**42.** 'Crime and Punishment' heroine
**44.** Carmen ___ ('The Producers' role)
**46.** Insincere ladies' men
**51.** Big name in calculators and digital watches
**52.** Eye affliction
**55.** Abel successor?
**57.** Animal-based scent
**60.** Capri, e.g.
**61.** 'Cheerleader' singer
**62.** He knows it all
**64.** Alabama's Civil Rights Memorial architect
**65.** Absence of oomph
**66.** Affectionate name for grandma
**67.** A.A. or AAA
**68.** Santa makes millions of them every Christmas
**69.** A stream might run through it

## Down

**1.** Actor Edward James ___
**2.** Billiard table cloth
**3.** Recite
**4.** Big-time brat
**5.** Colorado NHL team, in sports pages
**6.** Bananas or crackers
**7.** Aneurysm cause
**8.** Accessory for many a telecommuter
**9.** Airy, in music
**10.** Abbr. at the end of a planner
**11.** British P.M. before Gladstone
**12.** A, in geometry
**13.** N.Y.C.'s F.D.R. Drive, e.g
**18.** Five-sided pods
**22.** Bad check passer
**24.** Afflicts
**26.** Brit. money
**28.** Academy recognition, informally
**29.** Metal-bending tool
**30.** Agcy. issuance
**31.** Div.
**34.** Do a theater job, informally
**35.** A minimus is a little one
**36.** Passing
**37.** Dark-skinned grape used in winemaking
**39.** A dance, when repeated
**40.** Actress Layne
**43.** Contact information symbols, nowadays
**45.** A room with a view
**47.** Bahamas getaway
**48.** Shakes awake
**49.** Ascendant
**50.** Of a plant pore
**53.** Actress Graff
**54.** Big name in food wrap
**55.** Aeronautics achievement
**56.** Abu Dhabi bigwig
**58.** Automatic introduction?
**59.** Cable-___ sweater
**62.** Form of music files on the Net
**63.** Bears

## Across

1. Bodybuilder's bane
5. Barter, in Britain
9. Country from which the name 'Buttigieg' comes
14. A lowercase 'f' on a blue background, for Facebook
15. John of pro wrestling
16. End of the small intestine
17. Baseball's Hank
18. Italian naturalist Francesco
19. Big rush
20. St. Paul's twin
23. Be visibly disconsolate
24. Any of seven won by Betty White
25. Battler of Godzilla
27. Blue boys?
30. Big name in British art
32. Heyerdahl title start
33. 'Frost at Midnight' poet
37. Setting up production factories, e.g
41. Choice of salon treatments?
42. Andy Warhol portrait subject
43. African language
44. Scatters
47. Gets a grip on
50. 'All hail, Macbeth, ___ shalt be king hereafter!'
51. Arbiter with a whistle
52. Hack job?
58. A unit of geological time
60. Former Nebraska senator James
61. Affectedly cute
62. Soviet secret police chief
63. Baltic dweller
64. 'Das Rheingold' goddess
65. Cast off from the body
66. A bit sore
67. Angiogram necessities

## Down

1. Deception
2. 'A League of Their Own' actress Petty
3. Ancient Greek contest
4. Yelena ___, Soviet dissident and wife of Andrei Sakharov
5. Gets outta there fast
6. Given to crying
7. Japanese folk music with a swing feel
8. Aid for sandcastle builders
9. Bismarck's river
10. A high mountain
11. Boxer restraint
12. After-class aide
13. Amorphous creature
21. Energy expressed in volts: Abbr.
22. Drive ahead
26. City of southwest Yemen
27. A screech may accompany it
28. Common campus health diagnosis
29. 'Back up' PC command
30. Doughboy's ally
31. 'Ah me!'
33. Lit ___
34. A little change
35. Act like a beaver
36. Alphas might clash over them
38. Cities, informally
39. Disappearing communication system?
40. Invasive plant with yellow flowers
44. Crude house
45. 'Aww'-inspiring one
46. Like a well-worn dirt road
47. Aquatic bird
48. Fix a new exchange rate for
49. Before, of yore
50. Faithfulness, in a wedding vow
53. Acting colleague of Boris and Lon
54. A CFO is one
55. All wrong
56. Decide not to keep
57. Large green parrots
59. Gender prefix

# No. 77

## Across

**1.** Arafat's opening? (Var.)
**5.** Barn door fasteners
**10.** Bad grades
**14.** Ex-Spice Girl Halliwell
**15.** A little snowy, perhaps?
**16.** A choli is worn under it
**17.** Indecisive
**19.** Capital of the Swiss canton of Valais
**20.** Decorated, as leather
**21.** Alienate
**23.** Certain plane delivery
**25.** Abura-age ingredient
**26.** Cagers collect them
**29.** Central position
**33.** Kurylenko and Korbut
**37.** "A pocketful of ___ . . ."
**38.** American dogwood
**39.** Being nothing more than
**40.** Abbr. at a tire shop
**41.** Enameled metalware
**42.** A Beatle's last name
**44.** Actress Hurley, for short
**45.** A miner test?
**46.** Buzz producer
**47.** A Hatfield, to a McCoy
**49.** Rest time: Abbr.
**51.** AAA handout
**56.** Hastily thrown together
**61.** Bishop's chair
**62.** Hindu god of death
**63.** Attire for astronauts
**65.** Fluffy mass
**66.** Act like a volcano
**67.** Cave, in literature
**68.** Attach to a plow, in a way
**69.** Ending with electro-
**70.** Avec's opposite

## Down

**1.** Aggravated feeling
**2.** Choisy-___ (Paris suburb)
**3.** A dropped pop-up, e.g
**4.** Backhand a grounder, e.g
**5.** Bad luck
**6.** Aid in punching
**7.** Change direction abruptly
**8.** Adopt-a-thon adoptees
**9.** Cancels a correction
**10.** Christopher Hitchens and Marcel Proust, for two
**11.** 'April Love' composer Sammy
**12.** Animal symbol of fertility in ancient Egypt
**13.** Angle ratio
**18.** Feudal drudges
**22.** Cowboy in a sack?
**24.** Badly bruised
**27.** Certain antibody
**28.** Usurper
**30.** Creador del universo
**31.** Actress Ward
**32.** A low card
**33.** City in SW Russia
**34.** Duke Ellington's 'I ___ Song Go Out of My Heart'
**35.** Austrian city where Kepler taught
**36.** Highflying industry
**43.** Abbey ___
**45.** Ladies' maids in India
**48.** Certain Bach compositions
**50.** Bernoulli family birthplace
**52.** Bust targets
**53.** Actress Kelly
**54.** Austrian composer Bruckner
**55.** Annoyers
**56.** Cable network with a rhyming name
**57.** Composer Edouard
**58.** Berserk
**59.** Able to move nicely
**60.** Aachen abode
**64.** Cost-of-living fig

# No. 78

## Across

**1.** 'Broad City' actress Jacobson
**5.** A tot may have a big one
**8.** Brand promoted by Carrie Underwood
**13.** Barely flow
**14.** 'Bad!' sounds
**16.** Adventurer Amundsen
**17.** Actress Steppat of 'On Her Majesty's Secret Service'
**18.** Alternate for butter
**19.** Bases of civil suits
**20.** Activity for bored students and office drudges
**23.** Dish served on a skewer
**24.** A.L. Central city
**25.** Texas school
**28.** Person likely to have a big closet
**33.** A patient response?
**36.** Ace Attorney character Maya
**37.** Begetting
**38.** Bioethicist's stance
**41.** Gene who played Laura
**42.** Blazing, as the eyes
**43.** A cause for Steinem
**44.** Beach bird
**45.** They must be obeyed
**49.** A storm heading: Abbr.
**50.** Average of tre and nove
**51.** Belly bulge
**55.** What the shaded bends in this grid represent
**60.** Librettist for Verdi's 'Otello' and 'Falstaff'
**62.** Cartoon 'Yuck!'
**63.** Aids for football kickers
**64.** Expressions of approval
**65.** Abandon a position
**66.** A Bronte
**67.** With sickly pallor
**68.** 'u serious?'
**69.** Asian flatbread

## Down

**1.** Adidas rival
**2.** Abzug of the National Women's Hall of Fame
**3.** Affect strangely
**4.** Common emetic
**5.** Carefully pack (away)
**6.** Actress Fisher
**7.** Lacking detail
**8.** A freshman humanities course
**9.** Addlebrain
**10.** Bread spread
**11.** A keyboard key
**12.** Abbr. by a golf tee
**15.** Architectural column base
**21.** Arizona pol Jon
**22.** Battle of Trenton mercenary
**26.** Actor Ed
**27.** Actress Price who co-starred on CBS's 'Rules of Engagement'
**29.** Insult or injury
**30.** A driver may hit it
**31.** Belt along
**32.** Athletic great whose name and jersey number rhyme
**33.** At a fast clip, poetically
**34.** Ancient Greek metropolis
**35.** Like some methods of detection
**39.** A hasty escape
**40.** A Gershwin
**41.** A third of nove
**43.** Electrode in a transistor
**46.** Areas explored by submarines
**47.** A.L. East squad
**48.** Beachgoer's acquisition
**52.** Brandon ____ (Oscar-winning role for Hilary Swank)
**53.** Captive lady in 'The Faerie Queene'
**54.** Bad ____ (Lower Saxony city)
**56.** 'Bye for now' in a text
**57.** 'Dawn of the ____ fingers ...': The Odyssey
**58.** Cherry-pick
**59.** Acne-prone
**60.** A violinist might use one or take one
**61.** River to the Volga

# No. 79

## Across

1. Childish claim
5. A vegan one might have nopales
9. Benedict XVI and Francis
14. A rock star, often
15. Adjective for Death Valley
16. Baby bug
17. Not the main food allotment for one on an intel mission?
20. Bag holder?
21. Biblical endings
22. Accomplish by economy, with 'out'
23. Be a couch potato, say
25. Ancient dynastic ruler, briefly
26. Address from a rev.
27. Thin protein thread
33. Apricot relative
34. A in French
35. Barack's first chief of staff
37. Peter ___, general manager of the Met
38. Acts the couch potato
41. A sculpture of a three-legged one is considered lucky in feng shui
43. Abbey brews
45. Actor Cage, casually
46. Benihana founder Rocky ___
47. Recipient of blank checks
51. Abbr. in car ads
53. Abby's late sister
54. Bro hello
55. AT&T Stadium team, on scoreboards
56. 'Children of the Tenements' author
58. Crème de ___
63. Estimates the value of property too highly
66. Bandleader Count ___
67. Author Robert ___ Butler
68. Break up with
69. Artist James
70. Druggist for whom some commercial pills are named
71. Suburb of Paris

## Down

1. Dishable item
2. Bit of ingéniosité
3. Big name in meatless burgers
4. A four-star meal it's not
5. Far from tacky
6. Actress Graynor
7. Ending with herbi- or insecti-
8. 'Blues Everywhere I Go' singer
9. Bandage coating
10. Alternative to soy or almond
11. White-collar profession?
12. Bring back, as memories
13. Better balanced
18. De ___ (afresh)
19. Baba au ___
24. Broncos center Gradkowski
27. Abbr. on Chinese menus
28. Intestinal neighbors of jejuna and ceca
29. What the beat cop didn't want to be?
30. Medieval fiddle
31. Country singer Rimes
32. Area of South Africa
36. Be behind the success of
39. Conforms with
40. German composer Robert
42. Board mem., maybe
44. Less abundant
48. Land of ancient Ephesus
49. Certain camera support
50. Affordable German car
51. Acrobat developer
52. Renaissance dance (Var.)
57. Airtight tower
59. Insect nests
60. Shih ___ (diminutive dogs)
61. Adjusts lengthwise, as a skirt
62. Annual athletic award
64. 'A Rainy Night in ___' (1946 hit)
65. A perk-me-up?

# No. 80

## Across

1. Artist Picasso
6. Abner's artist
10. 'America's Got Talent' lineup
14. Giant furniture stores
15. Abstainer's opposite
16. Hockey player Kovalchuk
17. Nickname in James Fenimore Cooper tales
20. A keyboard key
21. 'Away with you, you varmint!'
22. Uninteresting types
23. Egg creator of note
26. A room with una vista?
27. One on the other side
32. 'Better safe than sorry' and others
34. Alternatives to trackpads
35. Africa's ___ Tomé
36. Armor plate that protects the chest
37. Action verb that's also a Roman numeral
38. Amazon Fire TV competitor
39. Abbess, e.g
40. A 'South Park' kid
42. Green ghost in the Ghostbusters movies
44. Picture displayed on a [circled letters] surface
47. Alexandra of 'Chicago Med'
48. Broadway title character who runs off to Atlantic City
51. Comply with a peace treaty, maybe
54. A son of Archie Manning
55. Aunt or uncle, e.g.: Abbr.
56. In a remarkable way, to a Jordanian?
60. Novelist ___ Thanh Nguyen
61. A bank may hold it
62. Bill of cowboy legend
63. All the ___
64. Animated Shrek
65. Far from fashionable

## Down

1. Bed for some kebabs
2. Cub leader
3. Vocal percussion
4. A GPS coordinate: Abbr
5. City in Kyrgyzstan
6. Radioactivity units
7. Abbr. in some job titles
8. A cat or a dog might be one
9. Matter-of-fact
10. Cowboy Troy
11. Ad agency award
12. Actress Daly
13. Becomes less taut
18. A couple of rounds in a toaster?
19. Actress Webb or Sevigny
24. Anglican's cousin: Abbr.
25. Dash initialism
26. Pixy ___
28. Ammonia derivative
29. Form of strength training
30. Alcoholic beverage often served warm
31. A musical might be on one
32. Cobble or patch
33. About three-fourths of la Tierra
37. Abe Lincoln's wife
38. As good as it's going to get?
40. California mission founder Junipero
41. Mandolin effect
42. Blemish on one's reputation
43. Former White House adviser Nofziger
45. Black marketeer in 'Casablanca'
46. Connected to the Internet
49. Ultimate object, to Aristotle
50. Alex's mom on 'Family Ties'
51. Software creators, for short
52. Showy flower of the iris family
53. A cherry may be served with it
54. Battenberg's river
57. Big ___ (large truck)
58. Alphabear, e.g
59. Actor Stephen

# No. 81

## Across

1. Citrus coolers
5. Airbag activator
11. Alphabet trio
14. After everyone else
15. Epicure
16. Au courant, once
17. Supplementary
19. Accept eagerly, with 'up'
20. Alluring quality
21. Actor Will of 'The Waltons'
22. Barzini and others, in 'The Godfather'
23. Egyptian temple complex near Luxor
25. Cow component
27. Bell ringer
32. Actress Gabrielle
33. Manner, in Marseilles
34. High, in German names
38. Break in the workday
41. Antarctic cruise sight
42. Bring in for another checkup
44. Commanded right
46. Practice that yields mixed results?
51. Annoyed state
52. Aches (for)
55. Actress Kathryn of 'WandaVision'
57. Actress Thompson et al
60. Angel in the outfield
61. An avis lays them
62. Like an air-filled lifeboat
64. Airline pilot's record
65. Actress ___ Nicole Brown
66. Above average in height
67. Lead-in for "light" or "night"
68. Acts like a ham?
69. Archaeological handle

## Down

1. 'Alas and ___'
2. Accomodations along the Black Sea
3. Fort's steep slope
4. 'A Sentimental Journey' author
5. Basis for a raise
6. 'A Clockwork Orange' instrument
7. Astringent target
8. Farewells overseas
9. Dante translator John
10. Abbr. before a number
11. Algae-killing chemical
12. Academic bigwig
13. Actor Omar
18. At the head of one's class
22. Alpha Cygni
24. Certain unit of heat, for short
26. Alternative to 'x,' in math
28. Sumerian sun god
29. Barely burn
30. 'Bien ___!'
31. Sheep in its second year
34. Another Tolkien creature
35. Explorer aboard the St. Peter
36. Internal passageways
37. Amber is a fossilized one
39. Artichoke heart?
40. Actress and inventor Lamarr
43. A.B.A. member's title
45. Counts calories
47. Brand with a Precisionist line
48. Brought (in), as a fish
49. Airport near Tokyo
50. Singer Josh
53. Dummy letters in ciphers
54. Burial stone
55. "Felix ___" (George Eliot title)
56. Acknowledge
58. Certain choir singers
59. Ensign on TV's 'Enterprise'
62. Burlesque star Lili St. ___
63. Anatomical foot

## Across

1. Aromatic hydrocarbon derivative
5. Acting ensemble
9. Butcher shop purchase
14. Address used among Friends
15. A khan
16. Black thrush
17. Anagrams piece
18. Actor Malek
19. "Awesome!"
20. Traitorous
23. Bit of a comic
24. Advertising element
25. Anti establishment?
27. Darer's question
30. Monetary unit of Nigeria
32. Certain petty officer: Abbr
33. Landing spots
37. Deviant, in a way
41. Barbecue delights
42. Animal home
43. Big name in air conditioning
44. Eminent scholar
47. Jewish calendar starter
50. Breed of terrier
51. A guitar may be connected to it
52. Babble
58. Beat, biblically
60. A unicycle has one
61. Acquire information, in a way
62. Costa Ricans, in slang
63. Animal fat
64. Barak of Israel
65. Apotheosize
66. African cobras
67. As authorized

## Down

1. Alaskan island
2. Nose: Prefix
3. Alarmed cry
4. Country singer Womack
5. Appetizer tray tidbit
6. A second time
7. Idiot (var.)
8. Mathematical physicist Peter who pioneered in knot theory
9. Bach's Brandenburgs, e.g.
10. Amber, for example
11. An inedible orange
12. Bee's landing place
13. Arduous journeys
21. Auto racer Fabi
22. Belfast residents
26. A lot of Tijuana
27. Johann who wrote the Swiss national anthem
28. Car that's seen better days
29. 'Always in motion is the future' speaker
30. Analogue of Lot's wife in Greek mythology
31. A bunch of them make a circle
33. Abecedarian phrase
34. Chichen ____ (Mayan city)
35. Nuclear binder
36. Aberdeen fellow
38. Bug-B-Gon maker
39. Christmas superlative
40. "I'll take ____ check"
44. Clay targets
45. Birthplace of Robert Burns
46. Made a quick change
47. Aesthetic judgment
48. Commingle
49. Star in Virgo
50. Cart
53. Adobe abode, perhaps
54. Ancient name of Asia's Amu Darya river
55. Prime minister who gave his name to an article of clothing
56. Being the reason for
57. Arnold of country
59. 'My mama done ____ me'

# No. 83

## Across

1. Mandlikova of tennis
5. Boston fish dish
10. Certainly not certain
14. 'The Adventures of ___' (European comics series)
15. 'An old silent pond / A frog jumps into the pond / Splash! Silence again,' e.g
16. Actress Kunis
17. Bald?
19. Alka-Seltzer sound
20. Jordan's prime minister
21. They may be penciled in
23. Catalog anew
25. Bit of Sinatra improvisation
26. A real mouthful?
29. Cameo shapes
33. Extend awkwardly
37. Actor Ferrigno
38. Beauty brand
39. A wolf may have one
40. Checkup sounds
41. Become understood, with 'in'
42. Al Jazeera viewing audience, mostly
44. 'America' contraction
45. English-speaking Caribbean island
46. Form of Sanskrit
47. Diode-inventing Japanese Nobelist
49. Belly, in babyspeak
51. Change from B to A, say
56. Snarky sort
61. Adjusted
62. Doig of TV's 'Andromeda'
63. Places where land meets sea
65. Cassini of fashion
66. Afghan capital
67. Baja boy
68. Be a sign of
69. Certain curtains
70. Bear a lamb

## Down

1. Bill of "Barry"
2. Classic dress style
3. Friendly goblin in Scandinavian folklore
4. Country singer Hoyt
5. 'Dallas' actress ___ J. Wilson
6. Instance, in Évreux
7. Acclivity
8. Half of an informal affirmative
9. Dressed to the nines, with 'up'
10. Be a make-up artist?
11. Baklava pastry
12. Act like lava
13. Barks sharply
18. In need of paving
22. Benefit or blessing
24. Be empathetic
27. 'Left ___ own devices ...'
28. Cavalryman of old
30. Hebrew for 'spring'
31. Director Riefenstahl
32. Barneys rival
33. A Belgradian
34. A Dumas
35. Actor's goal
36. Market maneuvering
43. Bambi's tail
45. Actor Bruce who played Watson
48. Pelvic exercises
50. Ball wear, at times
52. Bad for picnicking
53. Another nickname for the Governator
54. Beyonce's role in "Dreamgirls"
55. Pelé's given name
56. Annoying roommate, maybe
57. Drama intro?
58. Abruptly dismissed
59. 'Arms and the Man' playwright
60. Buckwheat noodle
64. Alternative to a bare floor

# No. 84

## Across

**1.** Auto performance factor, informally

**5.** A milliner makes it

**8.** Big name in scholastic philosophy

**13.** 'Deus ___' (1976 sci-fi novel)

**14.** Abbey brews

**16.** A crowd, it's said

**17.** Michael who played Worf on 'Star Trek: The Next Generation'

**18.** Chi follower

**19.** A real mouthful?

**20.** Arnold Schwarzenegger, Robert Patrick and Kristanna Loken?

**23.** Big name in food service

**24.** Indonesian island group

**25.** Gender prefix

**28.** Warning

**33.** Bit of a comic

**36.** Abbr. on some statements

**37.** Contract principal

**38.** End a split

**41.** Big name in fake fat

**42.** A.L. East athlete

**43.** Adolescent lead-in

**44.** Abbr. after 'Rev.' or before 'dev.'

**45.** Things that go bump in the night

**49.** A O doesn't have one

**50.** Absorb the cost of

**51.** Alamogordo's county

**55.** Native name for the Iroquois Confederacy

**60.** Amos Alonzo ___, coach in the College Football Hall of Fame

**62.** Composer Edouard

**63.** Anjou alternative

**64.** Clark Kent, originally

**65.** Airplane wing measure

**66.** Cheese type

**67.** Errant, to Burns

**68.** Awacs component: Abbr

**69.** Deviations of a ship's course

## Down

**1.** Alternatives to walks

**2.** Absentee ballot

**3.** Bazaars

**4.** A Finger Lake

**5.** Actor Jon of "Good Omens"

**6.** Et ___ ("and others")

**7.** 'Doctor Who' actor David

**8.** Actress Miranda

**9.** 'A Song for the Lonely' singer

**10.** Symbols on the flags of Algeria and Azerbaijan

**11.** Leak sources, perhaps

**12.** 'Big whoop'

**15.** Actress Belafonte

**21.** A shower curtain hangs from one

**22.** Fights

**26.** Apt to stay put

**27.** Bed or home attachment

**29.** Beveled for joining

**30.** 'A Chorus Line' number

**31.** Belt along

**32.** Autos originally from Oxford

**33.** Feel (for)

**34.** Office chair from Herman Miller

**35.** Merchants' meeting place

**39.** Able leader?

**40.** Amsterdam of l'Océan Indien, e.g

**41.** Brother of Dori and Nori in 'The Hobbit'

**43.** Grabs some chow?

**46.** Erse speakers

**47.** 'Am I talking ___ wall?'

**48.** Short and thick

**52.** Bomber ___ Gay

**53.** Adjust the tailoring

**54.** Roman banquet room

**56.** 'A Death in the Family' author

**57.** Beyond homely

**58.** Antiaging cream brand

**59.** About half of all deliveries

**60.** Bouncy Jamaican music

**61.** A touching game

# No. 85

## Across

1. Ad-libbed singing
5. Adult German male
9. Canadian blockhead
14. Met soprano Berger
15. Avoiding the draft?
16. Caesar's peepers
17. Sarge's 'Sell my city bonds!' telegram?
20. Operatic baritone Antonio
21. Beans go-with
22. Meaning of an embossed 'S,' maybe
23. Accented approval
25. A Fleming
26. A word to Virginia
27. What the shaded bends in this grid represent
33. Heifetz's teacher
34. Alexander ____, pioneer and early head of New York's subway system
35. Inept fool
37. Actress Karrueche
38. Commercial lead-in to Sweet
41. All wrapped (up)
43. Cold, in Cabo
45. Aware of what's what
46. A "Peter Pan" meanie
47. Larva-to-adult transition
51. River in Irkutsk
53. Abbr. akin to "alias"
54. Anger or fury
55. Dynamism
56. Advanced
58. Chemical used as an emollient
63. Has nonspecific opinions, e.g
66. Beach house feature
67. Elocution phrase
68. Hall-of-Fame college swimming coach ____ Thornton
69. Ancient city at the mouth of the Tiber
70. Acting too hastily
71. "A Letter for ___" (1945)

## Down

1. A century in Washington: Abbr.
2. Animal on a preppy shirt, for short
3. A dozen mesi
4. A social grace
5. Bank of New York founder
6. 'A Nightmare on ___ Street'
7. Accept another tour of duty
8. 'Bal du Moulin de la Galette' painter
9. Pop artist David
10. Andean stew vegetable
11. Secondary arrangements
12. Actress Kemper of 'Unbreakable Kimmy Schmidt'
13. Cambodian cabbage?
18. Ally of the Missouri
19. A theocratic republic
24. A shade of beige
27. Academic benchmark
28. Area to defend
29. Treaty violation, maybe
30. A Keebler elf
31. Big name in lawn care
32. Actress Rene
36. A quarter of acht
39. 'Anti' artist's nickname
40. Move closer to
42. A gaming platform for Mario
44. Ear malady
48. Soapberry tree
49. In a ___ of speaking
50. 'A half-filled auditorium,' to Frost
51. Architectural ellipse
52. Pueblo Indian structures
57. Sandal brand
59. A in German class?
60. Black Sea arm
61. Actress Austin
62. Alberto Azzo was a noted one
64. Aishwarya of Bollywood
65. Aides at M.I.T. and U.S.C

# No. 86

## Across

1. Wheel stopper
6. Boston ___ (orchestra)
10. A convertible's is removable
14. Beautiful maiden
15. Sun-swallowing demon of Hindu myth
16. A primary source for Scandinavian mythology
17. Drive to drink?
20. Beau Brummell
21. 'Aladdin' character who's transformed into an elephant
22. Becomes an Elvis impersonator?
23. Crick who co-discovered DNA's structure
26. Aid for one going places?
27. Woman presiding at a banquet
32. Longfellow's Hiawatha, e.g.
34. Acqua ___ (cause of annual flooding in Venice)
35. A meticulous person might pick one
36. Apiary residents
37. Abbr. for an open slot
38. An Aleutian island
39. Aid in making one's move?
40. 'A Hard Road to Glory' writer
42. Coins in India
44. Like electrical signals in the body [Toyota]
47. Adopted son of Claudius
48. Illegally seized
51. Bygone currency
54. Alternative to oil
55. 'u serious?'
56. Involving risk
60. Absolutely enthralled
61. Chum in chaps
62. An Italian cuisine
63. A waiter carries plates on it
64. Arizona birthplace of Cesar Chavez
65. A Dutch master

## Down

1. Grain husk
2. Accept for payment
3. One getting same-day medical service, maybe
4. Chartres shout
5. Baht : Thailand :: ___ : Laos
6. Moderator of Tribal Councils on TV
7. Aiea locale
8. A sorority letter
9. Get by (on)
10. Injure again, as a ligament
11. Beagle in the funnies
12. A gym may have a strong one
13. Adorers
18. Mikhail Gorbachev's first lady
19. App for posting pics
24. Cribbage one-pointers
25. Avian call
26. Bob of 'Home Again'
28. Actress Normand of the silents
29. Fictional ship on a five-year mission
30. 'Only joking!,' to a texter
31. Boarding spots: Abbr
32. 'Like, duh!'
33. Actress Stapleton
37. Actor ___ James of the 'Divergent' films
38. On ___ (commensurate)
40. Alpine crest
41. Feisty
42. Ballet ___
43. Director Grosbard
45. Coal, gas or wind can supply it
46. Angola's capital
49. Brighten the spirits of
50. A Thomas from Wales
51. Bog buildup
52. Abbr. for an MIT grad, perhaps
53. Ancient colonnade
54. Antiseptic target
57. Author Santha Rama ___
58. Ability to jump high, slangily
59. Alley rodent

# No. 87

## Across

**1.** Added conditions
**5.** Barney Fife, e.g
**11.** British scale divs
**14.** Baby bird's sound
**15.** Amsterdam in New York
**16.** A Dada founder
**17.** Every governor of California, while in office
**19.** A Greek letter
**20.** Fatty liquid
**21.** Big Apple restaurateur Toots
**22.** Dino's tail?
**23.** Relayed
**25.** Concrete reinforcement
**27.** Some Sunday broadcasting
**32.** Able to be halved equally
**33.** Andrea Doria's domain
**34.** Actor LaBeouf
**38.** Having a line of symmetry
**41.** T. J. ___
**42.** Brit's greeting
**44.** Alejandro's eyes
**46.** Perceiving what is not there
**51.** Bashkir's close cousin
**52.** Eastern hospice
**55.** Amish community project
**57.** Dora the Explorer's purple squirrel friend
**60.** City on Ishikari Bay
**61.** Flavor of some purple ice cream
**62.** Removes salt from
**64.** 'Aloha nui ___'
**65.** Early computer
**66.** Barber's blunder
**67.** 'Close ___ no cigar'
**68.** God with a broken tusk
**69.** Arm images, for short

## Down

**1.** Lhasa ___ (dogs)
**2.** Aussie Wimbledon winner ___ Fraser
**3.** Covered, in a way
**4.** Ariel or Tinker Bell
**5.** Alabama's Wilson ___
**6.** Abbr. after some telephone numbers
**7.** Cambodia's Phnom ___
**8.** Intact, in a way
**9.** Saharan nomad
**10.** Aluminum coin
**11.** Figure skater Witt
**12.** Dull color, in Düsseldorf
**13.** Appendage on a cowboy's boot
**18.** American chameleon
**22.** Bad place for witches, once
**24.** Gulf of Finland feeder
**26.** Act the mendicant
**28.** Annoy pettily
**29.** Atom with an electronic imbalance
**30.** A Chi-Town team
**31.** Abbr. on highway overpasses
**34.** Admonition in a movie theater
**35.** Mao's successor
**36.** Act cruelly toward
**37.** Actor Lane who voiced Mister Ed
**39.** Best-selling Steely Dan album
**40.** "An Iceland Fisherman" author Pierre
**43.** At lunch, say
**45.** 'American Idol' judge
**47.** Chain of connected ideas
**48.** Early film effect
**49.** Floating in the pool, e.g.
**50.** Ex ___ (as a favor, in law)
**53.** At attention
**54.** Features of narwhals
**55.** An onion is one
**56.** Leigh Hunt's '___ Ben Adhem'
**58.** Abode in the comic strip "B.C."
**59.** Spanish waves
**62.** Burrowed
**63.** Berliner's "I"

## Across

**1.** A famous Ali
**5.** 'Drag ___ Hell' (2009 movie)
**9.** Loy of filmdom
**14.** Give ___ for one's money
**15.** 'A touch more' sloganeer
**16.** Exclaimed surprise
**17.** Beginner's luck beneficiary
**18.** Schumacher of auto racing
**19.** Dante's 'La Vita ___'
**20.** Baskets, e.g.
**23.** Actress Susan
**24.** "And giving ___, up the chimney . . ."
**25.** Abalone-eating mammals
**27.** Ascribes, with 'up'
**30.** Aspirant, essentially
**32.** Albee's "___ and Yam"
**33.** One of The Three Tenors
**37.** Outlawing
**41.** Does in with a rope
**42.** Abbr. in many blood type names
**43.** Actress Amy with six Oscar nominations
**44.** Actress Milano
**47.** Baseball star nicknamed Godzilla
**50.** Cleaving tool
**51.** A lungful
**52.** House person
**58.** Make money by conning
**60.** Amount not to care
**61.** All-Star Cubs catcher Geovany
**62.** An "M" in MGM
**63.** Garrison of tennis
**64.** Bard's black hue
**65.** In the back
**66.** Affixes one's John Hancock to
**67.** A bit of force

## Down

**1.** A dirty person may draw one
**2.** Daughter of Ned Stark on 'Game of Thrones'
**3.** Beachgoer's woe
**4.** From one end of a battery
**5.** Aquino's predecessor
**6.** Birthday greeting sent with a click
**7.** Anatomical tissue
**8.** 'Antigonae' composer Carl
**9.** Frightening-sounding houseplant
**10.** A person who is not a doofus
**11.** Half a state name
**12.** Adamant refusal
**13.** All in ___ work
**21.** Ballpoint fill
**22.** Birthstone following opal
**26.** A bit more than a jog
**27.** Banned refrigerants
**28.** Adult male deer
**29.** Abu Dhabi bigwig (Var.)
**30.** Alan and Nathan
**31.** Sheep genus
**33.** Acai tree
**34.** Altoids buys
**35.** A polydactyl cat might have seven on one paw
**36.** Actress Cadranel of TV's 'Lost Girl'
**38.** Calls from the kids
**39.** Circuitry coil
**40.** Author Marsh
**44.** Corn cakes that might be served with nata
**45.** Acapulco article
**46.** Agreed with
**47.** Basalt, once
**48.** ABC or NBC, e.g
**49.** All too familiar
**50.** Architect Gehry
**53.** 'Casablanca' extra
**54.** Alfred E. Neuman expression
**55.** Half a Melville title
**56.** Boatloads
**57.** Abstainer's amount
**59.** Abbey address

# No. 89

## Across

1. All ___ (really cool)
5. Barracks, e.g
10. Bacchanal
14. Abie's Irish sweetheart
15. Apply by massaging
16. Missouri representative Bush
17. Roadblock
19. Cart horse sound
20. Some acids
21. Top in temple
23. Divisions of a century
25. 'I reckon'
26. Ancient Americans
29. Massenet opera based on a Daudet novel
33. Checked, say
37. Astern
38. Bun net
39. Check the weight of
40. Actress Myrna
41. Armor-___
42. Italian autos, familiarly
44. 'Almighty' item: Abbr
45. Australian rock
46. California's ___ Beach
47. Arthur Murray instruction
49. Be punished (for)
51. Distiller Joseph
56. Diamond lane
61. Endocrinological prefix
62. Came up short
63. Some calls to the police
65. Jessica with an Oscar for 'Tootsie'
66. 'Get Smart' robot
67. Asian lang.
68. Group of two hidden backward in 'daydream'
69. Broke, perhaps
70. Bend in the wind

## Down

1. A, C and E, on a piano
2. Grown garçon
3. Base for food glazes
4. Brandon ___ (Hilary Swank Oscar-winning role)
5. Cropped up
6. Backside, in Britain
7. Act the flunky
8. Actress Merrill
9. A bouncer may deny it
10. Number of people in a room
11. Air maneuver
12. Get inside and out
13. Cry of fright
18. 'Pink Shoe Laces' singer Stevens
22. Disarrange
24. Barista's injuries
27. Brewing
28. Barbers
30. Amundsen's goal
31. Coating of frost
32. Action figures?
33. Become dry, maybe
34. Chopper-related prefix
35. Brush-___ (dismissals)
36. Ran wildly, as a buffalo herd
43. 'All My Children,' e.g
45. Adjective on taco truck menus
48. Rang out
50. America, for example, which has a 'Cup' named after it
52. Come to ___ with
53. Affirm again, as vows
54. Anatomical cavities
55. Covered with a moist, green growth
56. Assertive
57. At the opponents' field
58. Arcade giant
59. Michael's sister La ___
60. 'Let me think...'
64. A clown might get it in the face

## Across

1. Aids for police detectives
5. Bang up, e.g
8. Cartoonist Segar
13. A head
14. Certain congregation leader
16. Animals depicted on the Ishtar Gate
17. Certain choir singers
18. Adoring biblical trio
19. Berry farm eponym
20. Person that's pointed at
23. Bar buy?
24. Author LeShan
25. A traffic jam may change it, for short
28. They offer rates for automobiles
33. A.T.M. input: Abbr
36. An encouraging word
37. 'Ali' or 'A Beautiful Mind'
38. From Belgrade
41. Former Mercury model
42. Activity that may require a lift
43. Egyptian ___ (breed of cat)
44. "Applesauce!"
45. Classic Corvette alternatives
49. Actor Alastair
50. Baby boomers, with 'the'
51. Simpson and Starr
55. Student of fossil plants with scattered money from a shark?
60. Certain salmon (Var.)
62. Samoa's monetary unit
63. 'A Life for the ___' (Mikhail Glinka opera)
64. Northern California town once home to the palindromic ___ Bakery
65. Affront
66. Amala de Xango vegetable
67. Beauty entrepreneur Linda
68. Alternative to ChapStick
69. Alphabetizing, e.g.: Abbr

## Down

1. Aquatic barkers
2. A "Survivor" site
3. Metrical accent
4. Alternatives to wings
5. Actress Rogers
6. Everyone included, after 'to'
7. Rough around the edges
8. City in Nevada
9. Home field of the Eagles, familiarly, with "the"
10. One concerned with creature comforts?
11. Abbr. on some statements
12. Abbr. in an auction catalog
15. Accomplish incorrectly
21. Aware of what's what
22. Embroidery frame
26. Subject of this puzzle [and proceeding counterclockwise]
27. Accouterment for Fred of 'Scooby-Doo'
29. Bric-a-brac holder
30. Beach bird
31. A for Adenauer
32. 'Aww'-inspiring one
33. Aides: Abbr
34. Phifer of 'ER' and 'Lie to Me'
35. Came out on top
39. Bargain basement container
40. Alternative to Dem. and Rep
41. Avril follower
43. Capital of Swaziland
46. Bad demonstrations
47. Abbr. before a trade name
48. Brazilian coffee port
52. Dangerous
53. Alexander and others
54. Classic Fender guitar, for short
56. Benihana founder Rocky ___
57. Almost fat-free
58. Author Ijeoma
59. A close watch
60. Burlesque star Lili St. ___
61. Acapulco gold

# ANSWERS

## Puzzle #1

```
O T O H   C H E F   S Y S C O
N O L O   A E R O   P O W E R
C O U N T E R A R G U M E N T
E N O K I S   S T A T   E C O
    T U I   W I N   T I N
C O N T O R T I O N I S T
W E A R   A I N   K H A N
T U N E   E S T E R   E L A M
  F O A L   E R I   M K T G
  S T E E P L E C H A S E S
S U E   C A L   S K I
E S C   T R A I   S V E L T E
P H O T O S Y N T H E S I Z E
T E N O R   A U R A   S C A N
A D D I S   S K E W   A E R Y
```

## Puzzle #2

```
I N D U S   M E D I   R E G S
S I E N A   A D E N   A L L Y
E X C O M M U N I C A T I O N
R O O   E V A   L E N A P E
E N R O U T E   M U S E
  A M B A S S A D O R I A L
E N T A I L   P R E P   M H O
L A I N   M I S   A P I A
I R V   S H U E   S O R E S T
O C E A N O G R A P H E R
    S E R S   C R O S S E R
H A S S A N   K A A   O N A
O M N I D I R E C T I O N A L
R I O S   S A K I   P L A T E
N E W T   T H E A   S A L E S
```

## Puzzle #3

```
R O W E   M E A G R E   M O S
E G A N   A L L R E D   O X Y
P E R S O N A L I T Y   B E N
R E M I T   N I N A   C I R C
O S T L E R   D R O O L
  H E R E F O R D S H I R E
    I N T L   O O Z E D
A H E M   E P I C S   S E C O
M I L A N   V O I D
Y E L L O W B E L L I E D
  S I R E E   T O P I C S
C U B A   I A M B   N A D A L
A V E   I N T E R N E C I N E
D E R   N E L L I E   T O N E
S A G   G R E T E L   S N A P
```

## Puzzle #4

```
B L E H   A T E N   C E L L S
L O L A   T O G A   I D I O T
O L E Y   O P A H   N U E V O
C O M M O N P L A C E   G I A
    O W E S   A R D E N T
G N A W E D   D I N A R
L E N   R O S E M A R I E
U N D E R E S T I M A T I N G
T E A L E A V E S   P K G
  B U M P S   U N I S Y S
M O R E S O   S P E C
A G E   A N C H O R W O M A N
C R A B B   Y O L O   N A D A
K E M A L   A M I S   I Z Z Y
E S S I E   N O D E   C E E S
```

## Puzzle #5

```
A M P S   W A L S H   C P S
W O R E   A G A P E   H E A T
S E I N   L E G A L   A N N A
  S T A T I O N M A S T E R
S O O   G E N   W A R E S
K I N D E R G A R T E N E R
I L E U S   G O B S
P Y R E   T W I G S   M U S A
  B A E S   L E N I N
  P A L E O N T O L O G I S T
A R M A N   R E M   V I S
B I O D E G R A D A B L E
B O R E   N A N A S   O R T S
A R A N   U N T I E   A S H Y
S Y L   S T A N D   F E E D
```

## Puzzle #6

```
T O M   S C A R P   B A E
A L O U D   N A B O O   A D V
P L A N O   A B S C I S S A E
S Y B I L   P E C K   H E R N
  V O W S   I N C A S E S
S C L E R A   P S E U D
W H I R   X M A S   T O N Y S
I O N S   Y A Y A S   W O V E
M U N I S   R E S E   B E E K
  T E R S E   G R O S S O
O B L I Q U E   H O A X
V A L E   D I D O   T I F F S
I S O S C E L E S   I N U R E
T H Y   A L L E E   O G D E N
Z O D   D Y E R S   D I G
```

# ANSWERS

## Puzzle #7

```
O S S A · A G R I · S A N S A
H U E D · P R O M · T H E A S
M I S A P P R O P R I A T E S
S T E R E O · M A I M · W E A
· · · · R I M · L A U · O D D
F O R T U N E T E L L E R ·
E M E R · T O Y · · I L K A
U N A U · S W I N E · R I G A
· I S S A · N O N · O N U S
· S T R A I G H T E D G E S
T H U · A B B · O H M · · ·
O A R · B E E T · R I O T E R
T R I N I T R O T O L U E N E
A P N E A · I V A N · T A N G
L O G O N · A A R E · S L A T
```

## Puzzle #8

```
M A C A U · E D D O · B A S E
A C O R N · T O E D · E G O N
S T R A I G H T F O R W A R D
T E R · L Y E · R I A L T O
O D E S S A N · L A N I · ·
· S P I N E T I N G L I N G
D E P E N D · E A T S · N O A
E N O W · J N R · O D O N
A Y N · S M O G · R A R I N G
R A D I O I S O T O P E S ·
· S T R S · E C T O P I C
A R E T H A · P F C · O N I
M I C R O B I O L O G I S T S
A S C I · E C C O · O V E R S
L A L A · L A O N · T O D A Y
```

## Puzzle #9

```
C H A R · M A T H I S · S G T
R A B I · A R I A N A · T A W
O B S E R V A N T L Y · O B O
C L O N E · M A I A · I C E S
K A R Z A I · N Y A C K · ·
· B I L D U N G S R O M A N
· M Y N A · · U N A M I
A G E R · L A I N E · S N U B
C A M A Y · L A P P · · ·
T H U N D E R S T O R M S
· L I S L E · S O O T H E
U P A S · D A S H · S H R E D
R U T · Y E L L O W T A I L S
D R E · A S I A N A · I D L E
S I S · S T A G E D · R E A L
```

## Puzzle #10

```
S L A W · S C A R · O D E S A
L U P E · P I S A · L E V E L
A L P S · U N I T · Y E A T S
B U T T E R C R E A M · D A O
· I G G Y · U P K E E P
A L L E G E · R A D I I ·
T I O · N E U R A L G I A
T O U G H M I N D E D N E S S
A N D R E O T T I · T A T
· A B Y S S · R U S S K I
T I M B R E · O O Z Y ·
I V A · A R G E N T I N E A N
S I N A I · A L I T · D U R A
H E I N Z · F L O E · I R B Y
A D A G E · F O N D · C O S A
```

## Puzzle #11

```
F L A K · S L A V E · M A H I
R U I N · T O P E D · A V I D
E N T O M O L O G Y · N I N E
D A C T Y L · S E T L I S T S
A S H T R A Y · A U F · ·
· R E A D D · D O B B S
S T I C H · H A O · O L L I E
H O B O · O F F · D O E R
A P I N G · O O F · I S T L E
M I S T I · S E E M S ·
· E L F · D U S T M O P
E A R M A R K S · T E R E T E
A X O N · E N C H I L A D A S
D E N E · R O U E N · M A K O
S L I D · E X P W Y · P L U S
```

## Puzzle #12

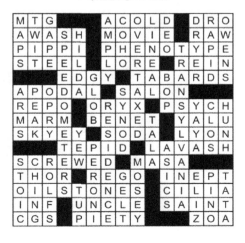

```
M T G · A C O L D · D R O
A W A S H · M O V I E · R A W
P I P P I · P H E N O T Y P E
S T E E L · L O R E · R E I N
· E D G Y · T A B A R D S
A P O D A L · S A L O N ·
R E P O · O R Y X · P S Y C H
M A R M · B E N E T · Y A L U
S K Y E Y · S O D A · L Y O N
· T E P I D · L A V A S H
S C R E W E D · M A S A
T H O R · R E G O · I N E P T
O I L S T O N E S · C I L I A
I N F · U N C L E · S A I N T
C G S · P I E T Y · Z O A
```

# ANSWERS

## Puzzle #13

```
P E T R . A N O A . A S T R A
A L O E . S O H N . C O H E N
C O N C E S S I O N A I R E S
E N I S L E . O D I C . E S E
. . . I R A . I S I . E E L .
O B S T E T R I C I A N S . .
H U L U . E N C . . S O C K .
S N I P . R O A M S . N O E L
. S P A T . . H O P . E R I E
. S C R E E N W R I T E R S .
M K T . E R M . N I K . . . .
O R I . F I B S . T E C H N O
N A T I O N A L I Z A T I O N
T U C C I . R I L E . R Y N E
E T H Y L . S P E S . L A I R
```

## Puzzle #14

```
S C E N A . A P S O . H A R M
A U X I N . G O A L . E R H U
C R O S S P O L L I N A T E D
K E N . . A U K . V A R I E D
S T E W A R T . Z I P S . . .
. R E C R I M I N A T I O N .
S P A R K Y . E N E S . M O A
P A T E . C S C . . U M P S .
A T E . I S A S . S A L I S H
S I D E S P L I T T I N G . .
. . N A I F . R E M A R K S .
R A G T A G . S U I . A N U .
O V E R C O M P E N S A T E S
M E N A . T A I S . O B E L I
P R O P . S A N T . L A D L E
```

## Puzzle #15

```
L A R B . A G N A T E . R I P
O M E R . T O O T O O . E D H
B A N A N A G R A M S . P E I
A R E C A . H A M A . M R A Z
R O S C O E . A S S A I . . .
. T O M M Y K N O C K E R S .
. I M A N . . H O V E L . . .
V E D A . A M A S S . S E X Y
E P O D E . R U L E . . . . .
T H U N D E R S H O W E R . .
. B A S L E . G E L A T I . .
A T T N . O V A L . L A P I N
J A I . S P E C I A L T I E S
A W N . A E R I A L . E D G E
R A G . C R E D O S . D O S T
```

## Puzzle #16

```
W H A P . G A L T . P R A H U
Y O U R . A L A R . R O M E R
L A T I . N O V A . I C I N G
E G O M A N I A C A L . S I E
. . A Y E S . M O S H E D . .
A P P L E T . C L A S H . . .
Y E A . . W H I T E W A S H .
L A C K A D A I S I C A L L Y
A L T A V I S T A . F E D . .
. L I S P S . D E C A D E . .
S Y R I A C . T A Y E . . . .
H O U . R O T I S S E R I E S
A D L A I . A N K H . E L M O
K E E F E . B R E E . A L U M
O R R I S . S O D S . L Y S E
```

## Puzzle #17

```
S H A D . O B O L S . S A P P
T O P E . C O W E R . P R E Y
A S S I S T A N T S . E A R L
G E I S H A . S O L V A B L E
Y A S M I N E . Y A K . . . .
. . M E N S A . N E S T S . .
A L M A S . Z I N . S A K A I
W I E N . Y E T . S O L A . .
E M I T S . M U M . X Y L E M
D A N I O . E R A S E . . . .
. P I T . N O N O I L Y . . .
P E T A L U M A . C O R N E A
E Y A S . T E R M I N A T O R
P E E T . S A M O A . N E R D
O S L O . I D Y L L . G R A S
```

## Puzzle #18

```
G Y P . S N I C K . B U B .
Y E A S T . C O C O A . L I L
M A R T I . A M E R I C A N A
S H E R M . L O S S . H I T S
. . A U L D . H E G I R A S .
A D M I R E . F E T O R . . .
B O O G . Y U L E . B O M B S
B L A H . S N O T S . P I A O
Y E N T A . T U S K . R E L Y
. E D G E R . U G A N D A . .
A B I D J A N . M A R C . . .
B A N G . V A P E . A T T I C
A L I E N A B L E . N O R V O
F O G . O G L E S . T R I E R
T O O . B E E B E . G Y N .
```

# ANSWERS

## Puzzle #19

| | | | | | | | | | | | | |
|---|---|---|---|---|---|---|---|---|---|---|---|---|
| C | H | A | V | | S | E | A | N | | S | M | I | R | K |

(Row 1: CHAV · SEAN · SMIRK)
Row 2: ROPE · ENZI · EERIE
Row 3: APPRENTICESHIPS
Row 4: BILBAO · ZOLA · DOH
Row 5: SRI · LIM · ENA
Row 6: PRACTITIONERS
Row 7: YECH · TAN · SECT
Row 8: MICA · ALKIE · TEAK
Row 9: DECA · ERN · INST
Row 10: POSTGRADUATES
Row 11: OFT · SOU · EEK
Row 12: BEA · ISLA · AEOLIA
Row 13: AMBASSADORSHIPS
Row 14: MULCT · GIDE · NESS
Row 15: AREAS · SEED · OVEN

## Puzzle #20

Row 1: PESTO · CASS · ADAM
Row 2: ALLER · ELHI · DULE
Row 3: COUNTERBALANCES
Row 4: EPI · XIA · KLATCH
Row 5: RECASTS · PIET
Row 6: ENTREPRENEURS
Row 7: PAGODA · YORE · NOW
Row 8: OBAN · SLA · SETA
Row 9: NET · UNTO · PUTNAM
Row 10: ELECTIONEERED
Row 11: HELP · TRITONE
Row 12: INCURS · PHO · RUS
Row 13: NEUROSCIENTISTS
Row 14: FARR · OREL · OBESE
Row 15: ORDO · NODS · REDON

## Puzzle #21

Row 1: CLAW · SCALPS · PTS
Row 2: RIMA · TAMARI · ROY
Row 3: INAUGURATOR · ELD
Row 4: SENSE · PHIL · ECUS
Row 5: PADANG · NOBLE
Row 6: AUTOBIOGRAPHY
Row 7: SAAR · ARTIE
Row 8: ZARF · DYADS · ASCH
Row 9: AKIRA · TOAS
Row 10: SUPERSPEEDWAY
Row 11: CUKOR · EASERS
Row 12: IZOD · LOPS · BINET
Row 13: MER · MALFEASANCE
Row 14: AID · PREFAB · GETA
Row 15: MTS · GASTRO · ODOM

## Puzzle #22

Row 1: CLEW · RICA · UPTON
Row 2: RAVI · ANAL · POOLE
Row 3: ERIC · SUMO · CARDI
Row 4: WALKTHROUGH · AIL
Row 5: EWEN · RACHEL
Row 6: CAPTOR · SKIRL
Row 7: OXI · RENEGADES
Row 8: MICROMANAGEMENT
Row 9: ESTIMATOR · BYE
Row 10: VICAR · BESTOW
Row 11: PREACH · KALE
Row 12: LEX · REMINISCENT
Row 13: AMICO · AVON · TRUE
Row 14: TALON · LOWE · OLDE
Row 15: OPENS · ERNS · REED

## Puzzle #23

Row 1: SLAP · TROON · SARS
Row 2: CLUE · AMOLE · THAE
Row 3: ROBERTSHAW · RAGA
Row 4: USENET · SYLLABUS
Row 5: BARSTOW · YAP
Row 6: COATI · CLOAK
Row 7: SLOSH · SUD · YERBA
Row 8: WART · ABY · SCRY
Row 9: ADEEM · BAL · OSSIE
Row 10: PASEO · ISLED
Row 11: PLY · SPEAKER
Row 12: PHANTASM · OTTAVA
Row 13: LOPE · BLOODSTAIN
Row 14: EWES · BURKE · ABAD
Row 15: XERS · AMISS · RANI

## Puzzle #24

Row 1: CHR · SCRAP · PRS
Row 2: OUIDA · HUEVO · HAH
Row 3: ORVIS · OBSESSIVE
Row 4: PLEAT · PEPE · PLED
Row 5: MOPS · ONBOARD
Row 6: EDMOND · KNOCK
Row 7: ZION · FAYS · CECUM
Row 8: RETD · STREW · SURI
Row 9: ASHBY · TISH · PENN
Row 10: AUDIE · EDESSA
Row 11: THICKET · MYER
Row 12: ROCK · CURE · ASSAM
Row 13: ARISTIDES · NOISE
Row 14: WAL · IDEES · ENNIS
Row 15: LEY · PESKY · GFS

# ANSWERS

## Puzzle #25

```
I N E S  ■  N A A N  ■  G E C K O
N A B E  ■  I S L E  ■  I L O N A
S T R A I G H T S H O O T E R
P L O U G H  ■  S T I R  ■  T E E
■  L T D  ■  E R G  ■  O L D
H A L L U C I N A T I O N
A L A E  ■  A L I  ■  O C T A
P E T A  ■  P I X A R  ■  H A R I
■  N E C K  ■  I C E  ■  R I A N
■  C H E S T E R F I E L D S
L A O  ■  I T O  ■  E I N
U M M  ■  S A S H  ■  N I K K E I
T W E N T Y S O M E T H I N G
S A R E E  ■  E V E R  ■  A L D O
K Y S E R  ■  D E T S  ■  T O E R
```

## Puzzle #26

```
A D D A X  ■  R O D E  ■  D A L I
L O R R E  ■  E C O N  ■  O D I N
P R O C R A S T I N A T I N G
E M P  ■  R H O  ■  O R N A T E
S A L I E R I  ■  O B I E
■  E N C A P S U L A T I O N
C R A N K Y  ■  I L E S  ■  N A E
R E V S  ■  B T U  ■  S E R V
O N E  ■  H S I A  ■  A V U L S E
P O S T O P E R A T I V E
■  O N A N  ■  N O N A G O N
S T E E D S  ■  S I M  ■  A D E
N O N C O M M I S S I O N E D
O R C A  ■  E O N S  ■  N U C O R
G A S P  ■  D O N A  ■  A R E N A
```

## Puzzle #27

```
P A B A  ■  A B O A R D  ■  P I O
E V E L  ■  R A P P E R  ■  R O B
C A L L I G R A P H Y  ■  I W O
K N I T S  ■  B L E U  ■  S E A L
S T E E L E  ■  A N A I S
■  F L A B B E R G A S T E D
■  S L U R  ■  R A L L Y
U S S R  ■  A N N A N  ■  L Y L E
G I M E L  ■  E G A D
H A U D E N O S A U N E E
■  G A T O S  ■  T E R R A N
S I G N  ■  T I T I  ■  P R A H A
C R E  ■  P A R A P H R A S E S
O M S  ■  O T I O S E  ■  T E A T
W A T  ■  W E S S O N  ■  A D D Y
```

## Puzzle #28

```
B A E R  ■  P A R K  ■  M U F F S
L I L A  ■  O D A Y  ■  U T L E Y
O W E N  ■  R O C A  ■  C A I R N
B A C K S T R E T C H  ■  T A G
■  L O I N  ■  R A S S L E
A T H E N A  ■  B L E C H
R A O  ■  D E A D H O R S E
T R O U B L E S H O O T I N G
A P P R A I S E R  ■  J U G
■  D R O I T  ■  D J A N G O
S A T U R N  ■  M O O N
O L Y  ■  E S T A B L I S H E D
M O N E T  ■  I D E M  ■  W O A H
A N E N T  ■  T A K E  ■  E L S A
S E R V E  ■  S K I N  ■  R I E L
```

## Puzzle #29

```
S E M S  ■  U K A S E  ■  A F A R
C L I P  ■  N E G E V  ■  L O B E
R E M I T T A N C E  ■  L U B E
A M E C H E  ■  I S R A E L I S
M I D Y E A R  ■  Y U M
■  S M E L T  ■  K A H L O
O M B R E  ■  F E E  ■  S N E E D
R A Y E  ■  U M S  ■  D A V E
G R E T A  ■  G U S  ■  V E D A S
S I R U P  ■  E R I C A
■  R E V  ■  E A T W E L L
T R A N S E P T  ■  G I R L I E
H A L E  ■  S E R V I C E M E N
A C M E  ■  P R E E N  ■  C A B O
R Y A S  ■  A M O N G  ■  K N E X
```

## Puzzle #30

```
B T W  ■  S H R U B  ■  A L F
R E E F S  ■  L E O N I  ■  C O O
A W A I T  ■  A R L I N G T O N
Y A N N I  ■  W O O T  ■  L I S T
■  G E M S  ■  D E B O N E S
O S W E G O  ■  R E D U B
F E H R  ■  A M E X  ■  Y E G G S
F L O P  ■  T A M E S  ■  T R O U
A L M A C  ■  T U S H  ■  R I B S
■  I C T U S  ■  U T O P I A
S P O N S O R  ■  D I E T
T I L T  ■  M A G E  ■  S T A L L
A P O S T A T E S  ■  S E R I O
P P G  ■  U T E R I  ■  A R T E L
H A Y  ■  N O S E S  ■  Y U L
```

# ANSWERS

## Puzzle #31

| R | O | J | O | ■ | S | A | A | B | ■ | T | H | I | O | L |
|---|---|---|---|---|---|---|---|---|---|---|---|---|---|---|
| A | E | O | N | ■ | E | L | B | A | ■ | R | A | N | G | E |
| S | I | D | E | S | P | L | I | T | T | I | N | G | L | Y |
| E | L | I | S | H | A | ■ | E | A | R | P | ■ | R | E | T |
| ■ | ■ | ■ | E | R | E | ■ | L | O | O | ■ | E | D | E | ■ |
| L | I | B | E | R | A | L | M | I | N | D | E | D | ■ | ■ |
| A | K | A | S | ■ | ■ | T | U | E | ■ | S | A | I | S | ■ |
| H | O | S | P | ■ | E | L | I | A | S | ■ | M | E | E | T |
| ■ | N | E | O | S | ■ | ■ | E | T | H | ■ | E | N | V | Y |
| ■ | R | O | L | L | E | R | C | O | A | S | T | E | R | ■ |
| E | C | U | ■ | O | I | L | ■ | O | W | N | ■ | ■ | ■ | ■ |
| P | I | N | ■ | V | L | O | G | ■ | C | I | C | E | R | O |
| S | E | N | S | A | T | I | O | N | A | L | I | Z | E | S |
| O | R | E | C | K | ■ | S | O | U | S | ■ | G | I | N | A |
| N | A | R | I | S | ■ | E | D | I | E | ■ | S | O | A | R |

## Puzzle #32

| S | I | E | G | E | ■ | G | U | M | P | ■ | M | E | M | E |
|---|---|---|---|---|---|---|---|---|---|---|---|---|---|---|
| T | O | N | E | R | ■ | S | T | A | R | ■ | A | T | U | L |
| U | N | D | E | R | S | T | A | T | E | M | E | N | T | S |
| N | I | A | ■ | P | A | S | ■ | S | E | N | A | T | E | ■ |
| S | A | N | G | R | I | A | ■ | S | O | S | A | ■ | ■ | ■ |
| ■ | G | R | A | N | D | S | T | A | N | D | E | R | S | ■ |
| K | N | E | A | D | S | ■ | T | Y | K | E | ■ | N | E | U |
| R | O | R | Y | ■ | V | A | X | ■ | ■ | O | G | E | E | ■ |
| O | R | E | ■ | U | S | E | D | ■ | T | R | I | A | L | S |
| C | O | D | E | S | W | I | T | C | H | I | N | G | ■ | ■ |
| ■ | ■ | ■ | X | I | A | N | ■ | L | A | N | K | E | S | T |
| A | S | P | E | N | S | ■ | P | E | W | ■ | M | I | A | ■ |
| T | H | O | U | G | H | T | L | E | S | S | N | E | S | S |
| T | O | R | N | ■ | E | R | O | S | ■ | P | A | N | T | S |
| S | E | T | T | ■ | S | I | D | E | ■ | A | N | T | A | E |

## Puzzle #33

| H | A | Y | S | ■ | M | A | R | S | H | A | ■ | M | A | S |
|---|---|---|---|---|---|---|---|---|---|---|---|---|---|---|
| A | L | O | K | ■ | A | D | O | N | A | I | ■ | E | L | K |
| L | E | G | I | S | L | A | T | O | R | S | ■ | U | K | E |
| T | R | U | D | I | ■ | H | E | R | A | ■ | S | N | A | G |
| S | T | R | O | D | E | ■ | T | R | A | C | I | ■ | ■ | ■ |
| ■ | T | O | R | T | O | I | S | E | S | H | E | L | L | ■ |
| ■ | ■ | A | C | R | O | ■ | ■ | K | O | R | E | A | ■ | ■ |
| I | B | I | D | ■ | H | A | W | K | E | ■ | N | E | W | B |
| N | A | M | I | B | ■ | ■ | A | M | T | S | ■ | ■ | ■ | ■ |
| C | H | A | M | P | I | O | N | S | H | I | P | S | ■ | ■ |
| ■ | G | E | S | T | S | ■ | ■ | E | L | O | P | E | S | ■ |
| H | U | I | S | ■ | A | M | I | D | ■ | V | I | L | L | A |
| U | R | N | ■ | P | L | A | N | E | T | A | R | I | U | M |
| S | E | E | ■ | C | I | N | E | M | A | ■ | O | N | T | O |
| H | A | R | ■ | S | E | I | Z | E | S | ■ | T | E | E | S |

## Puzzle #34

| C | O | T | S | ■ | M | A | M | A | ■ | D | E | N | Y | S |
|---|---|---|---|---|---|---|---|---|---|---|---|---|---|---|
| O | D | R | A | ■ | Y | M | I | R | ■ | E | X | E | A | T |
| M | E | I | R | ■ | S | O | N | G | ■ | A | T | A | R | I |
| B | R | O | T | H | E | R | H | O | O | D | ■ | M | E | L |
| ■ | ■ | ■ | R | A | L | E | ■ | O | B | V | E | R | T | ■ |
| I | T | S | E | L | F | ■ | T | O | M | E | I | ■ | ■ | ■ |
| O | A | K | ■ | ■ | C | A | R | P | A | C | C | I | O | ■ |
| T | R | A | N | S | M | I | G | R | A | T | I | O | N | S |
| A | N | T | I | V | I | R | U | S | ■ | ■ | O | C | C | ■ |
| ■ | ■ | ■ | T | E | T | E | S | ■ | C | L | O | T | H | O |
| E | R | S | A | T | Z | ■ | ■ | P | H | A | T | ■ | ■ | ■ |
| C | O | T | ■ | L | I | P | O | S | U | C | T | I | O | N |
| R | U | E | D | A | ■ | R | U | H | R | ■ | A | M | O | Y |
| U | S | A | I | N | ■ | A | Z | A | N | ■ | W | A | Z | E |
| S | E | L | M | A | ■ | M | O | W | S | ■ | A | X | E | S |

## Puzzle #35

| L | E | K | S | ■ | S | P | A | S | M | ■ | I | T | C | H |
|---|---|---|---|---|---|---|---|---|---|---|---|---|---|---|
| A | L | E | K | ■ | H | I | L | L | Y | ■ | N | I | R | O |
| M | I | L | I | T | I | A | M | E | N | ■ | U | R | E | Y |
| B | O | L | E | Y | N | ■ | S | W | A | N | K | E | S | T |
| S | T | I | R | R | E | R | ■ | ■ | H | I | T | ■ | ■ | ■ |
| ■ | ■ | ■ | E | R | O | S | E | ■ | P | I | T | C | H | ■ |
| T | H | O | S | E | ■ | O | W | L | ■ | S | T | O | L | E |
| Y | A | W | P | ■ | M | O | I | ■ | ■ | U | T | A | H | ■ |
| C | A | L | E | B | ■ | B | O | T | ■ | A | T | O | N | E |
| O | S | S | E | O | ■ | A | P | E | R | S | ■ | ■ | ■ | ■ |
| ■ | ■ | ■ | D | O | M | ■ | ■ | S | I | K | H | I | S | M |
| T | W | O | S | T | E | P | S | ■ | ■ | D | E | E | D | E |
| R | I | O | T | ■ | C | A | T | H | E | D | R | A | L | S |
| O | R | N | E | ■ | C | L | E | A | R | ■ | S | H | E | A |
| Y | E | A | R | ■ | A | P | P | T | S | ■ | H | O | S | S |

## Puzzle #36

| P | B | S | ■ | ■ | A | B | L | E | D | ■ | P | P | L |
|---|---|---|---|---|---|---|---|---|---|---|---|---|---|
| L | O | O | M | S | ■ | L | A | I | L | A | ■ | R | O | U |
| U | N | L | I | T | ■ | E | N | F | O | R | C | I | N | G |
| G | E | I | C | O | ■ | V | E | E | P | ■ | L | A | C | E |
| ■ | ■ | ■ | R | A | B | E | ■ | ■ | B | E | C | O | M | E | S |
| A | P | P | O | S | E | ■ | A | E | D | E | S | ■ | ■ | ■ |
| B | A | U | M | ■ | H | T | M | L | ■ | Y | E | C | C | H |
| L | Y | R | E | ■ | R | I | O | T | S | ■ | M | O | A | I |
| Y | A | L | T | A | ■ | M | U | S | H | ■ | O | A | F | S |
| ■ | ■ | E | U | L | E | R | ■ | ■ | A | M | U | L | E | T |
| I | N | B | O | X | E | S | ■ | G | N | A | T | ■ | ■ | ■ |
| T | O | R | R | ■ | N | A | S | A | ■ | P | H | O | N | O |
| C | R | O | S | S | O | V | E | R | ■ | L | E | V | I | N |
| H | I | D | ■ | O | R | E | A | D | ■ | E | D | U | C | E |
| Y | A | Y | ■ | D | E | R | M | A | ■ | ■ | M | E | X |

# ANSWERS

## Puzzle #37

```
I L L A █ S I L K █ W I Z E N
N E I L █ M O U E █ A L A L I
N O N T R A N S F E R A B L E
U N C O O L █ H I L T █ A E T
█ █ A L E █ R O I █ G R O
I N F I N I T E S I M A L
M O O R █ S T R █ E N I D
E I R E █ H E A R N █ N O U S
█ R E N T █ T A I █ A N N E
█ R E I N F O R C E M E N T
F L U █ M Y A █ A O N
E O N █ P E C S █ L O V A T O
S E N S A T I O N A L I S T S
T W E E N █ L U A U █ T O Y S
S E R A I █ E L M S █ A R L O
```

## Puzzle #38

```
F A H E Y █ P F C S █ M A G S
A N I M A █ R A I N █ A R I A
I N S U R R E C T I O N A R Y
N U T █ E A T █ D R I L L S
T S A R I S M █ R E B A
█ M E T A P H Y S I C I A N
F L I M S Y █ O A T S █ M I O
R E N I █ M S N █ U P D O
E X E █ O M E N █ R E S O A K
D I S C R I M I N A T E S
█ A L S O █ O N A S S I S
D E S P O T █ L U C █ I D K
U N C O P Y R I G H T A B L E
A B U T █ P O L A █ I D L E D
L Y M E █ E D I T █ A M E S S
```

## Puzzle #39

```
S C A M █ C H I M E S █ L O W
C O C O █ R O Y A L E █ O B I
U N I N S U L A T E D █ R O N
L O D G E █ D R A G █ O R E N
P R I O R I █ T I O G A
█ C L O C K W A T C H I N G
█ W E I R █ T A N I A
A P S E █ D A Y A N █ M E N O
B O T O X █ E V A L
S E I S M O G R A P H E R
█ P I L A U █ A A R O N S
W H E N █ K I R I █ S A O N E
H U N █ S T A I R M A S T E R
O R D █ K A N A K A █ E L K E
A D S █ A G A S S I █ R E A R
```

## Puzzle #40

```
S K A G █ S U D S █ P E R E S
H E I R █ A N Y A █ A D E P T
A N N I █ L I M N █ S A C C O
H O U N D S T O O T H █ T O W
█ G O A S █ A M B I T S
A C R O S S █ H U B I E
K O I █ F I B O N A C C I
I N C O N S I D E R A T I O N
O V E R E A G E R █ T O C
█ F A T S O █ J E K Y L L
T O M E T I █ J O V I
O V O █ N E U R O L O G I S T
M A R D I █ H A L T █ A B L E
B R O O K █ O K I E █ L O A D
S Y N C S █ H I E D █ I S M S
```

## Puzzle #41

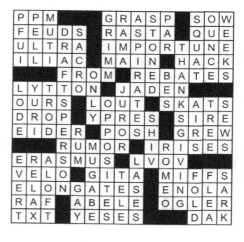

```
A C E S █ O C T A D █ I N D Y
S I M P █ U H U R A █ N O R I
I N D I S T I N C T █ F L A P
A C E T Y L █ S H E L L A C S
N O N S L I P █ D I U
█ P E S C I █ P E D A L
S M A S H █ Y I N █ S N I P E
W I L E █ O P S █ Z E U S
A K K A D █ P R Y █ F A U S T
G A Y L E █ S O N A R
█ S U S █ C L A R E T S
H O C K S H O P █ I T A L I A
T H A I █ E V A N E S C E N T
T E R N █ R E R U N █ K N E E
P R O S █ D R I B S █ S I S S
```

## Puzzle #42

```
P P M █ G R A S P █ S O W
F E U D S █ R A S T A █ Q U E
U L T R A █ I M P O R T U N E
I L I A C █ M A I N █ H A C K
█ F R O M █ R E B A T E S
L Y T T O N █ J A D E N
O U R S █ L O U T █ S K A T S
D R O P █ Y P R E S █ S I R E
E I D E R █ P O S H █ G R E W
█ R U M O R █ I R I S E S
E R A S M U S █ L V O V
V E L O █ G I T A █ M I F F S
E L O N G A T E S █ E N O L A
R A F █ A B E L E █ O G L E R
T X T █ Y E S E S █ D A K
```

# ANSWERS

## Puzzle #43

```
S P O T   E R R S   A R U B A
E T R O   N E A P   R O N A N
R U M P E L S T I L T S K I N
F I E S T A   S T O W   I D A
      A R M   E G O   N U S
T R A N S G E N D E R E D
S O F A   E N O   K I N D
K O R N   D U R O C   L E I F
  T I N O   S A I   A S S E
  K A F F E E K L A T S C H
O D A   F O X   S A R
P A N   S U E Y   N I E C E S
T E E T E R T O T T E R I N G
E G R E T   E G E R   S N O T
R U S T S   R I C O   T E S S
```

## Puzzle #44

```
A L B A N   M O C K   C A I N
M A A C O   E C H O   A L L E
P S Y C H O T H E R A P I S T
L E O   F E S   E L L I E S
E R N E S T O   G A G E
  E X T E R M I N A T O R S
S A T E E N   E R S E   C O E
A C I S   Q A T   K E A N
W A N   S T U N   T O W A R D
N I G H T W A T C H M A N
    O R I T   R E G I F T S
O U T R A N   J O T   R E I
I D E N T I F I C A T I O N S
S A T E   N O B U   O M N E S
E Y E D   G E E S   P O T T Y
```

## Puzzle #45

```
T A P A   S E E S A W   A T M
A P E D   E L L O R A   M A P
C A T E R P I L L A R   A X E
O C A L A   S E E R   B R I G
S E R I F S   M A S A I
  D E F E R E N T I A L L Y
    I L E X   T E L C O
O L A N   S P E C K   D O D D
R E B O P   R H Y S
V A L E D I C T O R I A N
  A L F R E   A G L E T S
S E T S   A T A P   M I S H A
F R I   P T E R O D A C T Y L
A M O   R E R I S E   E L M A
X A N   E R A S E S   S E E S
```

## Puzzle #46

```
T A M P   C O D S   S A M A R
A G E E   A B B E   H A O L E
L I R A   P E A R   E M C E E
C O U N T R Y S I D E   H U D
    U Z I S   U P P I T Y
S T A T U S   S P O D E
H I M   I N A M O R A T A
E P I S T E M O L O G I C A L
M I N I A T U R E   E X P
    B L A S T   S U N D A E
K I N S K I   J A M I
A L Y   B L O G O S P H E R E
T I A R A   L A K H   I B E X
E O L I C   P L E A   L E D A
S N A C K   E A S Y   O R E M
```

## Puzzle #47

```
J A D A   T Y C H E   I N C A
A B E D   R I L E S   N O O R
S A N D P A P E R S   S U N K
O S T E A L   M E E T I N G S
N E E D L E S   X I N
    P E P T O   C U T C O
P E P S I   A H L   K A R O L
L A I C   S I D   T E N G
A C E R B   M E M   A E T N A
T H R E E   S L A I N
    A R B   N A N O B O T
T R I M T A B S   M I K A D O
R E V E   B R O W B E A T E N
A M E R   K A W H I   P E L E
D O S S   A S S O C   I D L Y
```

## Puzzle #48

```
P V T S   P U L L S   P L U M
Y E O H   O L E A N   V E L A
R I D E   S M O K E S T A C K
O L D E S T   S E E K   V E E
    N O D   Z O N E R S
S T R A T O S P H E R E
H O Y   S C A L E   T U B B S
O P U S   G A L   F O R E
W O N K Y   A T L A S   R A P
  A R I S T O P H A N E S
W A R I E R   H U P
H U H   K O P F   A L E G A R
E G O M A N I A C S   D O M O
L I D O   E N L A I   O N Y X
P E A G   D E L T A   M O L Y
```

# ANSWERS

## Puzzle #49

```
I S A O . H A I R . H A W S E
N E M O . A R C O . O C H O A
T H I R T Y S O M E T H I N G
O R A T E S . N E S T . R I A
. . . S T A . R A E . L A N .
S P O N T A N E O U S L Y . .
H A V E . C T R . T A B U . .
E R E V . K E O G H . Z I T I
. A R I L . D A I . I R I S .
. . S N I C K E R D O O D L E
H O H . N A R . S E I . . . .
A M A . A S A P . O L I V E T
U N R I G H T E O U S N E S S
N I E C E . E T A T . D E S K
T A S K S . R E F S . O S O S
```

## Puzzle #50

```
D U D E S . H O L A . P R O F
A L E X A . A R A S . L O R A
U N C O N D I T I O N A L L Y
B A R . O R O . N O N F E E .
S E E T H E D . W A V E . . .
. P H O T O F I N I S H E R .
S M I R C H . L I T A . A P O
M O T U . S Y S . A M E S . .
T A L . U P O N . P L U S E S
P S Y C H O A N A L Y S T . .
. . H U S K . R O S T R A L .
A S S O R T . U N D . I S O .
B I O L U M I N E S C E N C E
A Z U L . E M I T . A R G O S
S E R A . N A S T . M A S T S
```

## Puzzle #51

```
G L O M . C O L A D A . I M P
N A R A . A M E L I E . N A H
A B B R E V I A T O R . F R Y
R I A N T . T H A N . L I E S
L A C I N G . I N J U N . . .
. . H E A R T B R E A K I N G
. . . S A R A . M A T E O . .
A K I N . D Y S O N . S I V A
N A D I A . A M O S . . . . .
T R A N S A T L A N T I C . .
. . H O L D S . A I R E R S .
T H O N . J E S T . C E L I E
B A A . B U T T E R K N I F E
S U N . U R S U L A . I C E R
P L S . S E E M L Y . C A R S
```

## Puzzle #52

```
B O Y D . E C C E . D A W N S
A T L I . A R O W . I X I O N
C H E N . M A L A . A L E R O
H O M E C O M I N G S . S A W
. . . R A N S . A P A T H Y .
O S B O R N . R E D O X . . .
B I O . . S E N O R I T A S .
I N S T R U M E N T A L I S T
S O C R A T I C S . . . D A Y
. . . A M I T E . A T H E N E
T A R M A C . U M B O . . . .
A W E . L A C E R A T I O N S
L A V A L . O Y E Z . S L U T
K R U P A . B E D E . T E N A
Y E E S H . B R O S . S A N G
```

## Puzzle #53

```
A M U R . S T O V E . A J A M
V I N O . P O K E Y . R E F I
I L L U M I N A T E . T E R R
S E E G A R . Y O R K I P O O
O R D E R E D . S I C . . . .
. . . G A I U S . D H A B I .
S P A C E . G N U . S O B E L
W A W A . E B B . K E E L . .
A L L E Y . S A P . N E R F S
B O S S A . T R A V E . . . .
. . . A W W . R U M M A G E .
S M I R N O F F . L E A D E D
L A T E . T A I L G A T I N G
U R S A . A T R I A . C E R E
G L Y N . N A M U R . H U E S
```

## Puzzle #54

```
W E F T S . S I M I . J A V A
H E L O T . C R A M . U N I X
E L I T E . H A S P . M I S O
T Y P E W R I T E R . P L A N
. . . . S U Z E . O B S E S S
F R Y E . C O S . V A T . . .
L E A P . H I T E . R A M P S
A D M I R E D . S P I R A E A
T O S C A . S I P E . T U R N
. . . U G G . M I L . S I T A
S N A R E R . P O E T . . . .
C O R E . E V A N G E L I S T
H U M A . G E N A . M A C H O
W R E N . G R E G . P I K E R
A I D S . S O L E . S T Y L E
```

# ANSWERS

## Puzzle #55

```
R A C K . T H U G . S W E A R
O Z I E . I O L A . H E N R I
B U T T E R F L Y F I S H E S
T R I O D E . A M E N . A P E
. . . A S A . E I D . R A N
P O S T M O D E R N I S M
A P P A . M I N . G O O P
D I E M . E N D O R . U N I V
. E L L S . E L A . C I T O
. L A C K A D A I S I C A L
C F C . H O T . F L O
O O H . M O R A . R O S I T A
O V E R O P I N I O N A T E D
R E C U E . A D D A . V E R D
S A K E S . L I E D . E M P S
```

## Puzzle #56

```
K O M B U . C H A W . L E W D
A L I A S . R O B O . E L E A
T E M P E R A M E N T A L L Y
H O E . I V Y . K O D A K S
I S O T Y P E . S I T U
. G R E E N S K E E P E R S
V E R E E N . T E R M . G I B
I P A S . T A D . A G F A
D I P . A L I F . B R I B E R
S C H A D E N F R E U D E
. S L A Y . A N N E A L S
M A S S I F . E S T . T O A
T R O U B L E S H O O T E R S
G A U R . E M M E . S A R A H
S U P E . T I E S . T E S L A
```

## Puzzle #57

```
S A B E . D E R M A L . F A A
L E A L . I N H E R E . I B N
A R R I V E D E R C I . L I T
D O R S A . S A M I . A L D I
E N E S C O . E N A R M
. L A U G H I N G S T O C K
. O L O F . P U R E E
P U R R . E D I C T . R E N D
I D I O M . L I A M
C O N S T E L L A T I O N
. G I N N Y . E N D E A R
A T T E . V O L E . T E R A I
Y A A . W I N E T A S T E R S
A M I . A E N E I D . T I G E
H E L . F R E S C O . E D H S
```

## Puzzle #58

```
R U D E . W E B B . C L O C K
O X E N . I V A R . R I S H I
B O S H . C E D I . E S K E R
B R E A D C R U M B S . A L B
. L U A S . E S T R A Y
T Y C O O N . A N G I O
Y A H . I N A U D I B L E
P R O C R A S T I N A T I O N
E N C O U N T E R . L O C
. A N K H S . S H T E T L
B R U T A L . S H O O
L O B . W E S T M I N S T E R
E L E N A . H A I M . S O R E
E L R O Y . O R Z O . U G G S
P O S T S . P E E N . P O S T
```

## Puzzle #59

```
S A C S . A R M C O . A T T Y
M I L O . V O W E D . N E U E
A M A L G A M A T E . C A B S
R E S O R T . H O U S E C A T
M E S S I A H . M U S
. P R O M O . E T H A N
S M O T E . M U R . D R I V E
L E H R . B R O . A L E X
I L E A C . R E Z . A L O S T
M E D I A . E X C O N
. N T H . O R G A N Z A
B L A S T O F F . E S P I E S
A U G E . D R A M A T I S T S
F R E T . A I R E D . S E A T
F E D S . D A M N S . H I S S
```

## Puzzle #60

```
D E V S . A R I . R O N D A
E X E C . J E S U . O T E R I
E T R O . A D A H . B O W E R
P O S T G R A D U A T E S
S L A T Y . O R C . W E E
. I N S T R U C T I O N S
T E D . T O A . L E M M A S
S N A F U E D . P A L P A T E
A N Y O N E . S E I . N E X
R U B B E R S T A M P S
S I R . E W E . I N S T A
. E N T R E P R E N E U R S
P L A Y A . A S I F . A N A S
P I K E R . T O F F . K N I T
L A S S E . N E S . S I N S
```

# ANSWERS

## Puzzle #61

```
T O O L _ H U T U _ P A B S T
O L L A _ O L I N _ R H O N E
L I E C H T E N S T E I N E R
L O O K U P _ E N U F _ E A R
_ _ F L A _ A N A _ S K Y
I N D E F A T I G A B L E _
N E E D _ T O D _ S I T H
D A C E _ E P E E S _ A T O M
_ L A M P _ A N I _ N E R A
_ P A R A L L E L O G R A M
H A I _ A C E _ R E D
A R T _ N E N A _ N E G A T E
W H A T C H A M A C A L L I T
K A T I E _ R A R E _ A V E O
S T E E D _ D S E D _ D A R N
```

## Puzzle #62

```
A W A R D _ S M U T _ F A S T
L O N E R _ K A T O _ A S K I
T R A N S L I T E R A T I O N
O T T _ O T A _ N E W A R K
S H O E P A C _ S A G A _ _
_ M E R C H A N D I S I N G
S H I L O H _ B O O S _ N I L
T E C S _ C O B _ S A B U
U M A _ L E H I _ B L O U S E
D I L L Y D A L L Y I N G _
_ U R I S _ E R A S U R E
S U B M I T _ O T O _ R E B
T E L E C O M M U N I C A T E
U L A N _ R E A P _ B A L E R
B E T S _ S I R S _ O N S E T
```

## Puzzle #63

```
K N U T _ A Z A L E A _ H E T
A I R E _ J A L O P Y _ O X O
S C A N D I N A V I A _ M I R
H A L L O _ Y N E Z _ Y E T I
A D I E U X _ T O G A S _ _
_ C Y B E R S T A L K I N G
_ T R A P _ O U T I E
U L V A _ O J E D A _ T E X T
R E A R M _ A B U D _ _
B U R E A U C R A T E S E
_ M A R N E _ H A H A H A
F O I L _ L A M A _ R O T O S
L O N _ T A S K M A S T E R S
U L T _ A C E T O L _ E R N E
B A S _ C E S S N A _ S Y S T
```

## Puzzle #64

```
B A J A _ S T A B _ P A L P S
A R P S _ A R C A _ A G O R A
A N E W _ B E C K _ T O R U N
L E G I S L A T U R E _ A D D
_ R U E D _ O N Y X E S
P S A L M S _ S K A T E _
A U G _ P L A C E N A M E
P L A I N C L O T H E S M A N
A U S T E R I T Y _ B I Z
_ T R U E S _ G I G O L O
L L O Y D S _ S I L L _
L A L _ C H E A P S K A T E S
A B A C O _ U N U M _ D O T H
M A N O R _ L I N O _ Y O U I
A N D R E _ A S K S _ S K I M
```

## Puzzle #65

```
B T U S _ C H O K E _ E L K S
L I N K _ H O U N D _ M O Y A
U N F O R E S T E D _ B A L I
R E I S E R _ A W A K E N E D
B A T H T U B _ S A D _
_ A B U J A _ E M B A R
S M A U G _ D A H _ L E E L A
C O I N _ D P I _ N E G S
U N R I P _ H A M _ S T R A P
D A Y N E _ A N S O N _
_ D E P _ A S E P S I S
N O N E S U C H _ T E A T R O
A J A X _ C L O V E R L E A F
R A V E _ C U T I E _ L A N A
D I E D _ I B S E N _ S K I S
```

## Puzzle #66

```
T E M P _ U L T _ M A H O N
E N Y A _ L O A M _ A G O N Y
N A R Y _ A E R O _ G E L E E
S C R E E N W R I T E R S _
E T H E R _ I L E _ T A E
_ S M O K E S C R E E N S
A C A _ P O S _ H E W I T T
B U R L A P S _ L I C E N S E
A L B E D O _ M A E _ S Y S
S P O K E S P E R S O N _
H A R _ E L M _ W E D G E
_ E N T R E P R E N E U R S
A R T O O _ B H A T _ D O I T
S O U R S _ S I L O _ E M M E
H Y M N S _ S E N _ R O M E
```

# ANSWERS

## Puzzle #67

```
A B B A . D E C I . E P S O M
L A O S . E V A N . L U C R E
A L P H A B E T I Z A T I O N
I M P A L A . O T I S . E N D
. . O R B . I N T . N O E . .
M E T E O R O L O G I S T . .
O R A N . E M O . C H I A . .
N I P A . D A N A I . A S C O
. K E C K . G U N . M T N S .
. S T A T I O N H O U S E S .
A M T . Y A N . T E D . . . .
L A R . A N G E . R E S C U E
T H I C K H E A D E D N E S S
A D E L E . S V E N . I R A Q
R I S E R . T E N T . T O R S
```

## Puzzle #68

```
R I A L S . N O G S . W O K S
A B B E Y . A L I A . H U L A
D I S E N F R A N C H I S E D
A Z O . L U V . H A T T E R .
R A R E B I T . D E L E . . .
. P A L E O B O T A N I S T .
E S T R U S . L E S S . N A Y
D A I N . H U S . . S C I E .
U G O . D A A E . E T O I L E
C O N C E N T R A T I O N . .
. A W N S . G U T T E R S . .
B I S S A U . L A D . R O T .
U N P A R L I A M E N T A R Y
S C A B . A S E A . E S T E E
T E R A . R A M S . P O E M S
```

## Puzzle #69

```
W A R P . U N E A S E . N E B
A V A R . L O L L O P . I D I
F E D E R A T I O N S . C O W
T R I S H . A M M O . T O M A
S Y S T E M . A M B I T . . .
. H O U S E T R A I N I N G .
. M E W S . T A N Y A . . . .
E B B S . C E A S E . S E X T
L E A P S . N O L L . . . . .
Y E L L O W J A C K E T S . .
. M A R I O . O C E A N S . .
S L I T . N Y A D . H A B I T
M A E . C O N S I D E R A T E
E M S . O N E I D A . E D E N
W E T . G A R M I N . D O R O
```

## Puzzle #70

```
A P P S . M O O K . C H I R P
G U R U . A L P O . L A Z A R
A M O R . C L E O . A D A M O
R A V I S H A N K A R . A I X
. M H O S . D I C K E Y . . .
S I R I U S . T R A S H . . .
W O O . L O U I S I A N A . .
A N T I I M M I G R A T I O N
T A I L C O A T S . M A D . .
. L E R O Y . S W I S H Y . .
L A M E S A . A K O N . . . .
U W E . H Y M E N O P T E R A
I N A N E . E W E R . A Y E R
S E R I E . D O L T . C R A T
A D A P T . E K E S . T A M S
```

## Puzzle #71

```
T H A W . E L B O W . O R B S
R A N A . M O L A R . B O L E
A N T I C I P A T E . S M U G
C O E V A L . S H A T T E R S
T I D E R I P . K E R . . . .
. P A I S A . A U G E R . . .
C H A R S . L A S . S C O R E
Y A R E . A H H . T U G S . .
S H U T S . F E B . E S T O P
T A M I A . S L I T S . . . .
. C U M . N O S I E S T . . .
P O P U L I S M . T A N N E R
R A U L . C H A T O Y A N C Y
O K R A . R E C U R . P I C S
D Y E R . O W E G O . T O O T
```

## Puzzle #72

```
G U R U . O C C . A D O P T
A T E N . C L O G . P I X I E
R E T S . T O L L . P L Y E R
T R A N S A T L A N T I C . .
H O R A E . I M E . O S O . .
. G R A N D P A R E N T S . .
R A G . A Y E . R I A T A S .
I N U T I L E . D I O R I T E
A G A S S I . R E N . N E O .
T U R K E Y B U R G E R . . .
A S A . A L I . C E A S E . .
. N O T H I N G B U R G E R .
A E T N A . G A E A . O U T A
C L E A R . H T M L . S E T T
A D E N O . E S T . E S S O .
```

# ANSWERS

## Puzzle #73

```
E R I S   D R I B   P L U S H
T O M E   I A G O   L O T T A
S U P P L E M E N T A T I O N
Y E S T E R   R O E S   L O D
      S E N   B E T   I D S
I M P R E S S I O N I S T
S O H O   E F T   C U Y P
M O O S   S W A R D   A M A N
  T S A R   L I E   V A R Y
  P S E U D O S C I E N C E
A A H   A D A   K E V
N G O   C O P S   N I I H A U
E A R T H S H A T T E R I N G
A M U S E   N A I L   O R A L
R A S P S   E G G Y   N O S Y
```

## Puzzle #74

```
C A R P I   L E F T   C A P S
A M E E N   I L I A   A V I A
D E F E N S E L E S S N E S S
D E L   A N Y   E P O C H S
O R E G A N O   O R I N
    C O N T R O V E R S I A L
E S T A D O   W I D E   M I C
F L I T   M I D   S P E D
T O V   S W A N   A G O R A S
S T E P P I N G S T O N E
    R O N A   I O N E S C O
O A T E R S   I L L   S E C
C R Y P T O Z O O L O G I S T
A G R A   M A N E   N O V A E
S H A Y   E K E D   O V E R T
```

## Puzzle #75

```
O B I T   A L C L A D   D A P
L A N E   V O L A R E   I R K
M I C R O S C O P I C   S E W
O Z A R K   O T T O   K R A Y
S E N O R A   O S S I A
  T R A I N S P O T T E R S
    S L O W   G E L E E
U T E S   S M A C K   R I G G
S O N Y A   G H I A
H E A R T B R E A K E R S
  C A S I O   I R I T I S
S E T H   M U S K   I S O L A
O M I   W I S E N H E I M E R
L I N   A N E M I A   N A N A
O R G   V I S I T S   G L E N
```

## Puzzle #76

```
F L A B   S W O P   M A L T A
L O G O   C E N A   I L E U M
A R O N   R E D I   S P A T E
M I N N E A P O L I S   S O B
    E M M Y   M O T H R A
S M U R F S   P A P U A
K O N   C O L E R I D G E
I N D U S T R I A L I Z I N G
D O O R N A I L S   M A O
    B A N T U   S T R E W S
G R A S P S   T H O U
R E F   C Y B E R A T T A C K
E P O C H   E X O N   T W E E
B E R I A   L E T T   E R D A
E G E S T   A C H Y   D Y E S
```

## Puzzle #77

```
A L E F   H A S P S   E F F S
G E R I   O W L E T   S A R I
I R R E S O L U T E   S I O N
T O O L E D   E S T R A N G E
A I R D R O P   S O Y
    F O U L S   M I D S T
O L G A S   R Y E   O S I E R
M E R E   P S I   T O L E
S T A R R   L I Z   A S S A Y
K A Z O O   E N E M Y
    S A B   R O A D M A P
S L A P D A S H   T H R O N E
Y A M A   S P A C E S U I T S
F L O C   E R U P T   G R O T
Y O K E   L Y S I S   S A N S
```

## Puzzle #78

```
A B B I   S I S   A L M A Y
S E E P   T S K S   R O A L D
I L S E   O L E O   T O R T S
C L O C K W A T C H I N G
S A T A Y   C L E   A A M
    C L O T H E S H O R S E
A A H   F E Y   S I R I N G
P R O L I F E   T I E R N E Y
A G L A R E   E R A   E R N
C O M M A N D M E N T S
E S E   S E I   O U T I E
  S T R E E T C O R N E R S
B O I T O   P T U I   T E E S
O K A Y S   S E L L   A N N E
W A N L Y   R L Y   N A A N
```

# ANSWERS

## Puzzle #79

```
D I B S | T A C O | P O P E S
I D O L | A R I D | L A R V A
R E C O N S I D E R A T I O N
T E A P O T | E T H S | E K E
| | V E G | T U T | S E R
M I C R O F I L A M E N T | |
S L O E | U N E | R A H M
G E L B | L O A F S | T O A D
| A L E S | N I C | A O K I
| A C C O U N T H O L D E R |
A P R | A N N | S U P
D A L | R I I S | M E N T H E
O V E R C A P I T A L I Z E S
B A S I E | O L E N | D U M P
E N S O R | D O A N | I S S Y
```

## Puzzle #80

```
P A B L O | C A P P | A C T S
I K E A S | U S E R | I L Y A
L E A T H E R S T O C K I N G
A L T | G I T | S H M O E S
F A B E R G E | S A L A |
| O P P O S I T I O N I S T
M A X I M S | M I C E | S A O
E G I S | M I X | R O K U
N U N | S T A N | S L I M E R
D A G U E R R E O T Y P E |
| G R E Y | N A N E T T E
D I S A R M | E L I | R E L
E X T R A O R D I N A R I L Y
V I E T | L I E N | P E C O S
S A M E | O G R E | P A S S E
```

## Puzzle #81

```
A D E S | I M P A C T | C D E
L A S T | F O O D I E | H E P
A C C E S S O R I A L | L A P
C H A R M | G E E R | D O N S
K A R N A K | U D D E R |
| P E R C U S S I O N I S T
| T A T I | T E N U E
O B E R | L U N C H | B E R G
R E S E E | G E E D |
C R O S S B R E E D I N G
| P I Q U E | Y E A R N S
H A H N | L E A S | T R O U T
O V A | C O L L A P S I B L E
L O G | Y V E T T E | T A L L
T W I | R A D I O S | A N S A
```

## Puzzle #82

```
A R Y L | C A S T | C H O P S
T H E E | A G H A | O U S E L
T I L E | R A M I | N E A T O
U N P A T R I O T I C | G A G
| N E O N | R E B E L S
W H Y N O T | N A I R A |
Y E O | A I R S T R I P S
S A D O M A S O C H I S T I C
S P A R E R I B S | Z O O
| T R A N E | S A V A N T
T I S H R I | S K Y E
A M P | I N C O H E R E N C E
S M I T E | A X L E | R E A D
T I C O S | S U E T | E H U D
E X A L T | A S P S | D U L Y
```

## Puzzle #83

```
H A N A | S C R O D | I F F Y
A L I X | H A I K U | M I L A
D I S T R E S S E D | P L O P
E N S O U R | E Y E B R O W S
R E E N T E R | D O O |
| T E E T H | O V A L S
S P L A Y | L O U | N I V E A
L E E R | A H S | S I N K
A R A B S | T I S | N E V I S
V E D I C | E S A K I
| T U M | R E G R A D E
S M A R T A S S | G E A R E D
L E X A | S H O R E L I N E S
O L E G | K A B U L | N I N O
B O D E | S W A G S | Y E A N
```

## Puzzle #84

```
R P M S | H A T | O C C A M
I R A E | A L E S | T H R E E
D O R N | M I N H | T E E T H
E X T E R M I N A T O R S |
S Y S C O | A R U | C I S
| A D M O N I S H M E N T
G A G | I N T | S I G N E E
R E U N I T E | O L E S T R A
O R I O L E | P R E | S T D
P O L T E R G E I S T S |
E N D | E A T | O T E R O
| H A U D E N O S A U N E E
S T A G G | L A L O | B O S C
K A L E L | S P A N | B L E U
A G L E Y | S Y S | Y A W S
```

# ANSWERS

## Puzzle #85

```
S C A T   H E R R   H O S E R
E R N A   A L E E   O C U L I
N O N C O M M U N I C A B L E
S C O T T I   P O R K   S I L
    O L E   I A N   Y E S
S T R E E T C O R N E R S
A U E R   O R R   Y U T Z
T R A N   N U T R A   S E W N
  F R I O   H I P   S M E E
  M E T A M O R P H O S I S
O K A   A K A   I R E
V I M   L E N T   O L E A T E
O V E R G E N E R A L I Z E S
L A N A I   E V A C   N O R T
O S T I A   R A S H   E V I E
```

## Puzzle #86

```
C H O C K   P O P S   R O O F
H O U R I   R A H U   E D D A
A N T I P R O H I B I T I O N
F O P   A B U   S N E E R S
F R A N C I S   V I S A
  T O A S T M I S T R E S S
O J I B W A   A L T A   N I T
B E E S   T B A   A T K A
V A N   A S H E   R U P E E S
I N T E R C E L L U L A R
  N E R O   U S U R P E D
P E S E T A   G A S   R L Y
E N T R E P R E N E U R I A L
A G O G   P A R D   P A S T A
T R A Y   Y U M A   S T E E N
```

## Puzzle #87

```
A N D S   D E P U T Y   K G S
P E E P   A V E N U E   A R P
S A C R A M E N T A N   T A U
O L E I N   S H O R   S A U R
S E N T O N   R E B A R
  T E L E V A N G E L I S M
    E V E N   G E N O A
S H I A   A X I A L   M A X X
H U L L O   O J O S
H A L L U C I N A T I N G
  T A T A R   I M A R E T
B A R N   T I C O   O T A R U
U B E   D E S A L I N A T E S
L O A   U N I V A C   N I C K
B U T   G A N E S H   T A T S
```

## Puzzle #88

```
B A B A   M E T O   M Y R N A
A R U N   A C E R   O O H E D
T Y R O   R A L F   N U O V A
H A N D I C R A F T S   D E Y
    A N O D   O T T E R S
C H A L K S   H O P E R
F A M   P A V A R O T T I
C R I M I N A L I Z A T I O N
S T R A N G L E S   N E G
  A D A M S   A L Y S S A
M A T S U I   F R O E
A I R   C O N G R E S S M A N
G R I F T   A R A P   S O T O
M E T R O   Z I N A   E B O N
A R E A R   I N K S   D Y N E
```

## Puzzle #89

```
T H A T   A B O D E   O R G Y
R O S E   R U B I N   C O R I
I M P E D I M E N T   C L O P
A M I N O S   Y A R M U L K E
D E C A D E S   Y U P
    I N C A S   S A P H O
C H O S E   A F T   S N O O D
H E F T   L O Y   C L A D
A L F A S   D O L   A Y E R S
P I S M O   S T E P S
    P A Y   S E A G R A M
B A S E P A T H   A D R E N O
O W E D   C O M P L A I N T S
L A G E   H Y M I E   P E R S
D Y A D   T A M E D   S W A Y
```

## Puzzle #90

```
S P I T   M A R   E L Z I E
E A C H   I M A M   L I O N S
A L T I   M A G I   K N O T T
L A U G H I N G S T O C K
S U S H I   E D A   E T A
  S P E E D O M E T E R S
A M T   T R Y   B I O P I C
S E R B I A N   M O N T E G O
S K I I N G   M A U   R O T
T H U N D E R B I R D S
S I M   R I A   B A R T S
  P A L E O B O T A N I S T
C O H O E   T A L A   T S A R
Y R E K A   S N U B   O K R A
R O D I N   E O S   S Y S T
```

Made in the USA
Middletown, DE
15 July 2022

69374127R10060